# DEMON-LOVERS
# AND THEIR VICTIMS
# IN BRITISH FICTION

# DEMON-LOVERS
## AND THEIR VICTIMS
## IN BRITISH FICTION

TONI REED

THE UNIVERSITY PRESS OF KENTUCKY

Scholarly publisher for the Commonwealth,
serving Bellarmine College, Berea College, Centre
College of Kentucky, Eastern Kentucky University,
The Filson Club, Georgetown College, Kentucky
Historical Society, Kentucky State University,
Morehead State University, Murray State University,
Northern Kentucky University, Transylvania University,
University of Kentucky, University of Louisville,
and Western Kentucky University.

*Editorial and Sales Offices:* Lexington, Kentucky 40506–0336

**Library of Congress Cataloging-in-Publication Data**
Reed, Toni, 1944–
  Demon-lovers and their victims in British fiction / Toni Reed.
    p.  cm.
  Bibliography: p.
  Includes index.
  ISBN 0–8131–1663–5
  1. English fiction—History and criticism.  2. Demonology in
literature.  3. Seduction in literature.  4. Victims in literature.
5. Women in literature.  6. Evil in literature.  7. Sex in
literature.  I. Title.
PR830.D38R4  1988
823'.009'353—dc19                                   88–18126

This book is printed on acid-free paper meeting
the requirements of the American National Standard
for Permanence of Paper for Printed Library Materials.
∞

# CONTENTS

Subtlety stalks in your eyes,
your tongue knows what it knows.
I want your secrets—I *will* have them out.
Seasick, I drop into the sea.
ADRIENNE RICH

# PREFACE

It is a widely accepted truism in today's world that women have never had the same degree of political, economic, and social power that men have enjoyed. Thanks to an unwavering vision, a belief in God-given equality, and hard work on behalf of countless women and men, we are beginning to see the faintest traces of acceptance of the revolutionary idea that women are as capable and deserving as men.

But we must still live with the legacy of the literature of oppression, designed to communicate the same underlying message over and over again, a message born of fear—that women must be controlled or destroyed so they will not become powerful and threatening to men. By looking at certain works of British fiction as if we had never read them before— and without the anxiety of influence that dogs any critic bold enough to reinterpret the writings of Emily Brontë, Thomas Hardy, and other distinguished British writers—we may discern a pattern I call the demon-lover conflict.

The demon-lover conflict is basically a struggle between misogynist and female victim resulting in her psychological or physical destruction. This pervasive pattern in literature reflects a social reality, one that we participants in that reality have not had the collective eyes to see and rebel against until the last twenty years or so. Historically, as long as women complied with the wishes of the dominant male-defined culture, they were safe. But women who deviated from their established and expected roles in the father-authored, husband-authored, son-authored, preacher-authored drama of life extricated themselves from the possibility of acceptance, love, support, and understanding supposedly found through conformity to prescribed "feminine" roles. They were, in fact, uniformly condemned and often destroyed. Demon-lovers in these stories willfully victimize women who have stepped outside the accepted perimeters of society in some way; metaphorically, both seduction and destruction take place in solitary places outside of civilization. Demon-lover tales all dramatize the social control imposed on women; these stories, furthermore, warn women against crossing the very distinct boundaries to which society conspires to hold them fast, lest all hell break loose. These boundaries—the tacitly agreed-to glue that has held society in check for generations—today are beginning to give way, thanks mainly to the impetus provided by the early women's movement and the Civil Rights movement and carried forward by millions of women, men, and children who have committed themselves to recovering from the damage that false notions and lies can do.

I would like to thank countless people who helped me directly or indirectly in the preparation of this book. First, I would like to acknowledge the invaluable assistance provided by Professors Daniel R. Barnes, Barbara Hill-Rigney, and Arnold Shapiro, who helped to shape the spirit of this work in its early stages. Without their support, encouragement, and astute criticism, this book would not have been possible. I also thank several other colleagues and friends for their interest in my project and for believing in my ability to lay bare the demon-lover conflict: Morris Beja, Richard Martin, John Gabel, Ruth Ann Hendrickson, Ann Hall, Pat Naulty, Cory Dillon, and Cheryl Carter. For their help, both professionally and personally, I am deeply indebted.

To my mother, Margaret Ann Reed, and my father, John Reed, I owe my sincerest gratitude for creating the kind of environment in which I could make up my own mind about the way the world is; and to my children, Kelly and Christopher Bates, I owe my thanks for their constant support and interest in this project.

I would especially like to thank the Midwest Modern Language Association and the University Press of Kentucky for co-sponsoring a book contest into which I entered my manuscript. MMLA and the Press are serving the world of scholarship in a highly commendable way.

Finally, I wish I could find the words to thank hundreds of people encountered over the years who have gently, or suddenly, or painfully, or unknowingly ripped off my blinders or demanded that I stop lying. To these people, and some of you know who you are, I will forever be grateful.

I lovingly dedicate this book to my mother, my first language teacher.

# ONE

# Woman Wailing
# for Her Demon-Lover!

Like one, that on a lonesome road
Doth walk in fear and dread,
And having once turned round walks on,
And turns no more his head;
Because he knows, a frightful fiend
Doth close behind him tread.

COLERIDGE,
*The Rime of the Ancient Mariner*

The body of literature for any period of history reflects, in part, the fears, conflicts, and ethical concerns inherent in the culture which produces its novelists and poets. Although the literary works of any particular century tend to reflect the social mores of that period and are therefore tied to historical interpretation, certain themes in fiction transcend the cultural milieu in which the works were formed. Certain thematic patterns or motifs continue to appear in literature throughout time, patterns that may in fact be traced from the earliest Greek myths through the Bible and influential works of fiction to popular literature and contemporary films.

Works of literature, including the earliest known forms of orally transmitted folklore, tend to repeat a finite number of plots or stories which captivate audiences generation after generation. In the same way children enjoy hearing the same fairy tales told over and over again, most people respond to tales that resemble others they have heard or have read before; familiarity with stories fosters personal identification, and identification by audiences leads to repetition of the same basic plot formulas over time. This study concerns itself with one specific narrative scheme which has been repeated since the beginning of literary history, yet one that has been largely ignored by scholars and literary critics: the demon-lover motif.[1] Briefly, this motif conveys in an exaggerated fashion an aggressive man's attempts to dominate and destroy a naive, impressionable woman and demonstrates also her lack of perception and foresight. The struggle takes on mythical proportions, in part because of the larger-than-life and often supernatural features of demon-lover figures, and in part because of the frequency with which the tale is told.

One of the earliest literary expressions of the demon-lover motif is found in "The Demon Lover," a popular ballad sung in Scotland and England as early as the mid-seventeenth century. In the ballad, a spirit or a cloven-footed revenant lover destroys his former mistress through supernatural means as revenge for her unfaithfulnsss to him while he has been away. In literary works as well, authors typically attribute demon-lover figures with supernatural traits that distinguish them from other characters. In fiction, the supernatural quality of the demon-lover—the mysterious charm and the perverse, dangerous impulses—establishes a direct parallel to the earlier ballad. The women in these works are both repelled by and attracted to the supernatural character of their demon-lovers. Very often the dark figures are compared to Satan, a powerful supernatural being, or are said to possess demonic qualities, and their behavior seems excessively cruel, even diabolic at times.

Myths of course are stories which represent beliefs held by a group of people; in ancient Greek and Roman cultures, many myths explained natural phenomena which could not otherwise be explained. In such narratives, human dramas are enacted on a cosmic scale through the mythology of a cultural group, dramas which often capture elemental struggles between the sexes. Conflicts depicted by mythological figures—for example, conflicts between Apollo and Daphne, Pan and Syrinx, and Eros and Psyche—symbolize struggles between men and women. As narratives evolved from the early mythology to folktales, ballads, and other forms of folk literature, these conflicts continued to be expressed because they parallel human experience. It is no surprise that formal written literature frequently focuses on the recurring human conflicts between men and women. By identifying the characteristics of one particular type of conflict, the demon-lover conflict, we may explore both its mythological and psychological dimensions.

Northrop Frye believes that "the structural principles of literature are as closely related to mythology and comparative religion as those of painting are to geometry" (*Anatomy of Criticism*, pp. 134-35). He provides some critical tools for discussing the relationship between literature and myth. Frye classifies literature into four groups of what he calls "mythical movements": romance, comedy, irony, and tragedy. Because works of fiction that express the demon-lover motif all conclude with personal disasters, they correspond most closely to what Frye calls "tragedy." He also divides the universe of discourse (and by extension the universe itself) into two basic modes, the apocalyptic and the demonic. The underlying theme or "structure of imagery" in any literary work he calls *dianoia* (p. 140). This term is useful for discussing works that share a thematic structure—e.g., the victimization of a woman by a man—which clearly places the collection of works under discussion in this study in the realm of the demonic, according to Frye's binary scheme. Moreover, Frye applies the term *mythoi* to mean "the generic narratives . . . which are these structures of imagery in movement" (p. 140). *Mythoi*, meaning plot, is useful in this study for identifying ballads and tales that share similar plot features, elements which tend to be repeated in works that may be grouped together as "demon-lover tales."

By applying the Aristotelian concepts of *dianoia* and *mythoi*, Frye provides a means of distinguishing between content and method. The literature discussed in this book expresses through a fairly predictable structural design a particular view of the "demonic" impulse in human beings as depicted by fictional characters. A demonic world view, according to Frye, presents a "world of the nightmare and the scapegoat, of bondage and pain and confusion" (p. 147)—a description which easily fits such works as "The Demon Lover" ballad, *Wuthering Heights, Tess of the d'Urbervilles, Dracula,* and many other works discussed in chapters 4 and 5.

Demon-lover tales all involve a struggle of wills, deception, and human destruction, and embody a recognizable plot formula. Certain works of literature, written centuries apart by authors who may or may not have known about similar works that preceded their own, may be grouped together according to theme and structure. Works that share a theme as well as a basic formulaic structure—for example, works identified as demon-lover tales—exist because they invoke universal human responses. Why the same stories are retold throughout literary history and how the germinal idea is disseminated are intriguing questions that will be addressed in the following chapters.

Richard Chase believes that myths represent primeval reality and that human beings repeat mythical thought patterns as a result of authentic aesthetic experience (*Quest for Myth,* p. vii), although he fails to account for the fact that several authors may independently share mythical images or patterns. Referring to Freud's theory of "the pleasure principle" and its relation to what he called the "repetition compulsion," Chase states: "He [Freud] believed that the repetition compulsion was a device employed by the organism to guard against psychic trauma, a device to set up a tension of modified fear . . . so as to prepare the psyche to meet sudden onslaughts of fright" (p. 101).

To Freud, according to Chase, the repetition of motifs, such as the one found in demon-lover stories, serves a practical psychological purpose: to help us brace ourselves against the possibility of painful emotional assault. Chase goes on to describe in greater detail the relationship between the mythmaker and the myth, reinforcing the idea that myths are indeed useful for anticipating trauma: "The act of projecting inner emotions into the outer world (i.e., the first act of mythmaking) is a self-protective measure. The finished myth may perhaps be considered, as Freud considers the painful kind of dream, a device for sending small and controllable armies of stimuli against the individual psyche as a repeated warning . . . " (pp. 101-2).

Chase seems to concur with Freud that as a repetitive dream often warns us of some danger, a recurring myth functions to protect us from some vague, imminent threat. The repetition of the myth provides a way for the mythmaker and for those who experience the myth over and over to achieve psychic equilibrium.

Contrasting the positions of Freud and Jung regarding the function of myth, Eric Gould writes: "He [Jung] suggests a radical departure from Freudian orthodoxy in his explanation of what the human mind does as it creates fictions, largely through his theory of the archetype. Freud used mythological tales as the expression of repressed instinctual drives in the unconscious. He treated these narratives as sources of dream material which derive from the infantile psychological life of man. Jung, on the other hand, finds in myth a mature psychological life, and isolates there certain primordial images: the shadow, the *anima* and *animus*, the wise old man, and so on" (*Mythical Intentions in Modern Literature*, pp. 15-16).

Whereas Freud attributes the human mythmaking consciousness to infantile urges, Jung asserts that myths comprise the fundamental structure of the unconscious mind. Jung explains the tendency for mythical thought patterns to reappear throughout literary history by suggesting that human beings share a "collective unconscious," psychic memories stored in the deepest recesses of our minds. The collective unconscious, Jung suggests, contains archetypes that were present from the beginning of time. According to Jung, the archetypes in literature stir us because they communicate essential truths via psychic images. In the following passage Jung defines his often-misused term "archetype": "The primordial image, or archetype, is a figure—be it a daemon, a human being, or a process—that constantly recurs in the course of history and appears wherever creative fantasy is freely expressed. Essentially, therefore, it is a mythological figure. When we examine these images more closely, we find that they give form to countless typical experiences of our ancestors. They are, so to speak, the psychic residue of innumerable experiences of the same type. They present a picture of psychic life in the average, divided up and projected into the manifold figures of the mythological pantheon" (*The Spirit in Man, Art, and Literature*, pp. 16-17). Viewed in Jungian terms, the demon-lover of both the folk and literary texts may be seen as an archetypal figure, a primordial image repeated throughout history because it resides in the human psyche and from time to time emerges in the form of concrete songs and tales.

Derived from Jung's theory of archetypes, archetypal criticism has played an important role in scholarly studies for many years. Frye, for example, attributes the basis of his own theory of archetypes to Jung. Pointing out the ease with which archetypes lend themselves to repetition throughout history, Frye states: "The fact that the archetype is primarily a *communicable* symbol largely accounts for the ease with which ballads and folk tales and mimes travel though the world, like so many of their heroes, over all barriers of language and culture" (p. 107). As a literary figure, the demon-lover circulated by way of Scottish and British folklore before being adapted by poets and writers. Frye's conception of archetypes as communicable symbols helps to explain why audiences identify with certain stories that are told and retold across the generations.

Maud Bodkin, one of the earliest literary critics to recognize the importance of Jung's work on archetypes for the study of literature, contends that poets communicate their visions of human experience, their interpretations of the world around them, through archetypal images which correspond to the emotional realities of their communities. "When a great poet uses the stories that have taken shape in the fantasy of the community," Bodkin remarks, "it is not his individual sensibility alone that he objectifies" (*Archetypal Patterns in Poetry*, p. 8).

Myth or archetypal criticism was firmly established by 1957 when Frye published *Anatomy of Criticism*, in which he states that archetypes are "associative clusters" or "communicable units" connecting one poem with another. Archetypal criticism, Frye proposes, is primarily concerned with literature as a mode of communication regarding social experience. By concentrating on conventions and genres, the archetypal critic attempts to integrate poems into the greater body of literature while discerning specific motifs, patterns relating to *dianoia* or *mythoi*, which characterize works of literature. By extension, archetypes connect one novel or piece of short fiction with another. By recognizing the demon-lover conflict as a pervasive leitmotiv in British fiction, we may better comprehend volatile gender relationships, interpreted by writers over the past four hundred years through archetypal characterizations.

The prototypical lover and victim were introduced by Samuel Richardson when *Clarissa* was first published in 1748. Other works—for example, *Wuthering Heights* and *Tess of the d'Urbervilles* in the nineteenth century and D.H. Lawrence's "The Princess" and Elizabeth Bowen's "The Demon Lover" in the twentieth century—repeat the basic aggression motif. The demon-lover figures that appear in these works share certain characteristics with the medieval concept of Satan, an observation which supports the idea that these works are thematically related. In all of these works the demon-lovers are dark, deceptive, obsessed men who possess or destroy their victims at night, much in the way Satan is said to behave toward his victims.

Chapter 2 traces the development of the concept of Satan, focusing on Satan and demons in general as "lovers" who seduce and destroy women, and establishes the similarity between the victimization experienced by "witches" and the women in the demon-lover tales. The ballad and the fiction on which the present study is based represent a demonic interaction between victimizer and victim. John J. White has remarked on the psychological effect that archetypal literature has on its readers because of historical or mythological associations: "A work of fiction prefigured by a myth is read in such a way that our reactions to character and plot are transformed by an awareness of the mythological precedent; it is a relation whose importance lies primarily in what it brings to bear on the act of reading and interpreting, not in any determining function it may have in respect of the actual plot. Prefigurations arouse expectations in the reader which may or may not be fulfilled, and in any case will probably be satisfied in unexpected ways" ("Mythological Fiction and the Reading Process," p. 77).

The mythological figure on which the demon-lover is based is clearly Satan. Recognizing the recurrence of the Devil figure in literature, Bodkin remarks: "If we attempt to define the devil in psychological terms, regarding him as an archetype, a persistent or recurrent mode of apprehension, we may say that the devil is our tendency to represent in personal form the forces within and without us that threaten our supreme values" (p. 223). Works of fiction based on the myth of Satan (or on the *reality* of the Devil for those who believe in the existence of personified evil) force us to examine our own potential for evil and confront us with our own vulnerability. Satan and women accused of witchcraft as recently as two hundred and fifty years ago represent the historical precedent for the demon-lover conflict. Stories related by women persecuted as "witches" by English magistrates (all men) are remarkably similar to the underlying plot structure found in the ballad: a demonic figure tempts, seduces, betrays, and victimizes women. As history, ancient mythology, the ballad, and the literary works reveal, women have been victimized since the beginning of human society.

Feminists today have much to say about the collective victimization of women by patriarchal societies as well as the victimization of individuals in the form of rape, spousal abuse, and spiritual and psychological oppression. But few feminists have commented upon the victimization depicted in works of literature considered exemplary by our culture. Schoolchildren, both boys and girls, have read *Wuthering Heights* (for example) for generations and have been intrigued by the unnamable passion they feel; as a result of their reading they have formed deep and lasting associations between passion and love: to love, in other words, means to suffer intensely, as Heathcliff and Catherine suffer as a result of their violent interactions. Thus, violence, passion, and love become fused in a drama of oppression. Literature depicting the oppression of females encourages the belief that "strong-willed men" must conquer women, while "weak-willed women" eventually succumb to the uncontestable power of men obsessed with possessing them. One possible explanation for the faithful perpetuation of the demon-lover motif is that historically men have had power over women and have protected that power by willfully subjugating women and, more, by possessing them. Perhaps the demon-lover conflict expresses the collective oppression of women, and as a body of literature represents a collective warning to women not to deviate from male-defined roles, for those who do are punished.

Feminist critics often write seething critical exposés about the damage done by patriarchal critics who have, over the years, consistently misunderstood, misrepresented, or dismissed the woman's point of view. Some feminist critics reinterpret literature; others attempt to undo misapplied critical theory; still others provide new paradigms for the study of literature that serve to equalize past critical practice. To a large extent feminist criticism has involved a search for myths that explain the social, psychological, emotional, and psychic experiences of women that would otherwise go unexplained.

In 1979, a time when women critics were still attempting to define feminist criticism and its mission, Sandra Gilbert and Susan Gubar took the literary world by storm by tracing fictional images of enclosure, represented primarily by Charlotte Brontë's Bertha Mason, "the madwoman in the attic." By giving poor Bertha, the silenced victim of social oppression, a voice, Gilbert and Gubar are able to deconstruct and contradict the Victorian image of woman as "angel in the house." By exploring patterns of patriarchal and domestic imprisonment reflected in women's nineteenth-century fiction, the authors expose previously unacknowledged passion, anxiety, and fury experienced by women during the nineteenth century, a time notable for its stereotype of women as complacent and domestic.

In *Archetypal Patterns in Women's Fiction*, Annis Pratt identifies several recurring archetypes expressed in women's fiction—"the green-world epiphany, the green-world lover, the rape trauma, enclosure, and rebirth" (*Patterns*, p. 170)—and connects the frequency of these archetypes to constricting gender-stereotypes. She contends that because women innately find solace in nature, they psychologically retreat from claustrophobic society by seeking or remembering pastoral settings, a green-world, where societal constraints are nonexistent and where they may "struggle for personal authenticity" (*Patterns*, p. 22). Sometimes into this nostalgic and private world, however, comes a green-world lover who leaves the mores and values of civilization behind, in a sense, to pursue a woman who contradicts or suspends the accepted norms of society. The conflict that invariably ensues is what Pratt calls "the rape-trauma archetype, . . . one of the most frequent plot structures in women's fiction" (*Patterns*, p. 5). The author recognizes the mythological importance of the pursuit motif when she states, "The plot line in which a rejected male continues to pursue an unwilling woman can be traced as far back as Greek mythology: Daphne turned into a laurel tree in order to escape Apollo, Syrinx became a reed to avoid Pan, Arethusa changed into a spring to elude Alpheus" (*Patterns*, p. 25). The pursuit motif, Pratt recognizes, extends throughout literary history, as many works of fiction repeat the same mythological conflict. In her discussion of *Wuthering Heights*, Pratt outlines Catherine's famous ambivalence towards social conventions. Heathcliff, "whose name suggests a natural landscape, takes on erotic and mythological fascination for Catherine," who responds by turning "away from 'appropriate' males toward fantasies of a figure, projected from within her own personality, more suitable to her needs" (*Patterns*, p. 22).

Pratt's suggestion that Catherine projects an image of a suitable lover out of her own emotional makeup is congruent with the underlying thesis of this book, and her focus on the green-world milieu of the demon-lover conflict is consistent with the ballad texts and literature under discussion, dramas which uniformly unfold outside of society. Pratt recognizes

Catherine's projection of a mythical figure, Heathcliff, as an extension of her own needs, although Pratt attributes Catherine's fixation on Heathcliff primarily to his association with nature and wildness. To be sure, Catherine is immediately fascinated with the wild gypsy-orphan from Liverpool, but she sees Heathcliff as a means of escaping from social conventions, from the accepted role a female must play in a male-dominated world. Following her stay at Thrushcross Grange, however, Catherine clearly feels ambivalent toward rebellion. Regarding the passion between Catherine and Heathcliff and Catherine's ambivalence that leads to her marrying Edgar Linton, Pratt comments:

> This tension between a hero's passion for an unacceptable lover and her dutiful marriage characterizes Emily Brontë's *Wuthering Heights*, where . . . Heathcliff takes on the qualities of the green-world lover archetype. The plot structure is determined by Cathy's overt conformity to gender norms in marrying the insipid Edgar Linton . . . while remaining attached to Heathcliff, her true lover. Cathy grows up torn between a desire to emulate the passive, spotless femininity of Edgar Linton's sister, Isabella, and her identification with the spirit of Heathcliff. Her transformation from a free existent to a young lady is only skin deep, of course, and *Wuthering Heights* is thus, among other things, an anatomy of the damage done to woman's psyche by repressive gender norms. [*Patterns*, p. 81].

Rather than seeking the solace of a green-world via Heathcliff, Catherine pursues danger, savageness, and ultimately victimization as well as her own death.

Although some women writers present characters who retreat from the pressures of ill-fitting social definitions, restrictions, and expectations by entering a green-world or its equivalent (however wild and savage), other women writers show women's assimilation into society as empowering (*Pride and Prejudice, Middlemarch, Mrs. Dalloway* are conspicuous examples). Male writers, too, represent the green-world as an escape from socially prescribed limitations. D.H. Lawrence's *Lady Chatterley's Lover* is, to use Pratt's phrase, a green-world tale with a green-world lover, but the stories identified in this study follow a particular plot formula that necessarily results in tragedy.

In *Woman and the Demon: The Life of a Victorian Myth*, Nina Auerbach acknowledges the centrality of a nineteenth-century myth of women as victims. She takes issue, however, with contemporary literary interpretations based upon a view of women as defeated, pathetic victims; instead, Auerbach insists that female characters who appear helpless and hopeless at the hands of would-be perpetrators are actually empowered through conflict. Regarding the transformation or reversal that magically occurs as a result of oppression, Auerbach writes: "But when we actually read *Trilby, Dracula,* or *Studies on Hysteria* we are struck by the kinds of powers that are granted to the women: the victim of paralysis possesses seemingly infinite capacities of regenerative being that turn on her triumphant mesmerizer and paralyze him in turn. Disposed and seemingly empty, the women reveal an infinitely unfolding magic that is quite different from the formulaic spells of the men" (p. 17). Victorious women, rather than victims, Auerbach asserts, "pervade the Victorian imagination" (p. 186). There is a certain power in powerlessness, she suggests, which provides an impetus for the transforming effect of oppression; thus, "the demonic angel rises from within the angel in the house" (p. 186).

The demon-lover conflict focused upon in the present study provides a means for exploring a particular type of archetypal conflict that occurs in certain identifiable works of British fiction and involves neither demonic angels nor angels in the house. These works, however, are grouped together because they all express, in a general way, similar plot structures. Identifying a group of works whose plots revolve around the oppression or destruction of women does not negate the literary or aesthetic value of the works but does provide a means of reinterpreting them in light of their mythological and historical contexts.

Many feminist critics are opposed to the applicaton of Jung's theories to literature primarily because of his propensity for reductionism, a criticism that needs to be addressed. In her essay "Dwelling in Decencies: Radical Criticism and the Feminist Perspective," Lillian S. Robinson captures the objection held by many feminists: "It seems to me that nothing could be more harmful to a coherent and fruitful reading of the 'literature of women' than Jungianism with its liturgical pronouncements about The Masculine and The Feminine—not to mention The Universal and The Innate" (p. 28). Annis Pratt, on the other hand, defends Jungian criticism, suggesting that Jung's theory of archetypes may be adapted to accommodate "the psycho-mythological development of the female hero" ("Archetypal Approaches to the New Feminist Criticism," p. 3).

There is no doubt that elements of Jung's theory, particularly his masculine and feminine archetypes, may be used by literary critics to justify and foster gender-based stereotypes. In his writings, however, Jung theorizes about the content of the human psyche, asserting that all of the archetypes that he identifies coexist in the unconscious realms of all human beings. Thus, the human psyche is androgynous, as both "masculine" and "feminine" images are accessible to the conscious mind under certain conditions, such as stress, highly creative moments, or a personal epiphany or recognition.

Authors such as Emily Brontë, Bram Stoker, and D.H. Lawrence shape certain archetypes into fictional characters, which helps to define the archetypes, and they explore the dynamics between representative parts of the human psyche, parts that may be in conflict. Archetypes, as described by Jung and brought to life by writers, duplicate identifiable features of society; archetypes and fictional characters, then, are not created in a vacuum but, instead, mirror reality. Demaris S. Wehr affirms the reflective quality of archetypes by stating: "Assimilation and integration of archetypal images can be understood as an experience of wrestling with the demons of a sexist culture. Gender-linked archetypes can be seen as inner representatives of socially sanctioned, seductive but oppressive, roles and behavior patterns" (p. 37). If archetypes found in works of literature reflect actual roles played in society, then the demon-lover conflict may indeed reveal the quintessential struggle between the sexes identifiable in our patriarchal culture, a struggle whose complete story may not be told until we first look point-blank into its face. Feminist critics have embraced the task of clarifying the effects of a male-dominated society on language, imagery, fiction, literary perceptions, and the courage to write. Catharine R. Stimpson reminds us that we must first uncover the underlying structure of oppression before we can change the anatomy of gender-linked persecution: "First, we cannot understand history, politics, and culture until we recognize how influential the structures of gender and sexual difference have been. Second, men, as men, have controlled history, politics, culture. They have decided who will have power, and who will not; which realities will be represented and taught, and which will not. In so doing, men have relegated women, as women, to the margins of culture, if not to silence and invisibility. We must also act, politically and culturally, in order to change history" ("Introduction," p. 2).

In the demon-lover tales, the heroines betray themselves, in a sense, as their lack of self-awareness and perception ultimately puts them at the mercy of unworthy rakes who victimize them. Vivid archetypal characters, though, clarify basic human interactions, in much the same way that mythological figures have done for centuries. Jung's theory of archetypes is useful for defining the psychological and psychic dimensions of an age-old conflict as it appears in literature. Jung's theory of the *animus* and the *anima*, usually the crux of the objections raised by feminists, is meant to explain the two sides of the human psyche; an individual's gender tends to correspond with the dominant side of his or her psyche, according to Jung, but everyone has both *animus* and *anima* to call upon. The ballad and the demon-lover tales reveal a drama based on characters who are exaggerated representations of the *animus* and the *anima*. The stereotypical demon-lover and victim exhibit characteristics that Jung associates with these often-misunderstood terms: the demon-lover is aggressive and cruel and the victim is passive and easily destroyed. With few exceptions, neither character proves admirable.

Jung's theory also helps to explain why the demon-lover motif has been as pervasive as it has been in both British and American literature over the past two hundred years. If Jung is correct in his scrutiny of the human psyche, then we human beings see ourselves—our innermost conflicts along with our social conflicts—reflected by these demon-lover narratives. It is no wonder, then, that as a misogynous thread running through literary history, the demon-lover motif stretches from the beginning to the present and no doubt will continue well into the future.

Dorothy Van Ghent (who should not be mistaken for a feminist critic) acknowledges the importance of the demon-lover archetype in British fiction. Richardson's *Clarissa* she sees as a work of literature whose basic mythlike structure neatly juxtaposes the power of the divine, represented by Clarissa, and the power of the demonic, represented by Lovelace. Van Ghent suggests that Emily Brontë utilizes the same mythic structure in *Wuthering Heights*: Heathcliff is an archetypal demon-lover and Catherine, though not so puritanical as Clarissa, falls victim to Heathcliff's obsessive passion. The integral structure of a literary work reveals meaning, and to Van Ghent, mythic form promotes subjective expressions of motivations, of emotions, and of spiritual values. To examine the dynamics of the aggressor/victim conflict in these two works, as well as in others, is to identify a myth which is fundamental to the human psyche.

In attempting to define the nature of American fiction, Leslie A. Fiedler has explored a number of aggressor/victim relationships. *Clarissa*, according to Fiedler, represents a class struggle between the bourgeoisie and the lower class—symbolized by Lovelace and Clarissa, respectively; in this case, the aggressor/victim relationship is the result of social class identity. Fiedler's comments regarding class struggle do not hold true for the demon-lover tales identified in this study. Hardy's Tess, for instance, is certainly of a lower socioeconomic class than Alec d'Urberville, but the same is not true of Catherine Earnshaw and Heathcliff. Along with many other critics, Fiedler does, however, recognize the importance of Lovelace as a prototype. "Lovelace is a Machiavelli of the boudoir," Fiedler states, "a Don Juan who turns monomaniac before the unconquerable virtue of Clarissa" (*Love and Death in the American Novel*, p. 63). Richardson was clearly intrigued by the power struggle inherent in the conflict that takes place when a determined seducer becomes obsessed with a virtuous woman. *Clarissa*, the first literary demon-lover tale, anticipated countless works of fiction whose informing principle is the life-threatening conflict between victimizer and victim, or what Fiedler calls "their fatal encounter" and "the archetypal act of Seduction" (p. 69). Fiedler recognizes the impact *Pamela* and *Clarissa* have had on the development of the novel when he writes: "The novel proper could not be launched until some author imagined a prose narrative in which the Seducer and the Pure Maiden were brought face to face in a ritual combat destined to end in marriage or death; the form and its mythology were born together, in the works of Samuel Richardson" (p. 62). Richardson wrote *Clarissa* during a time when "The Demon Lover" was circulating widely in Scotland and England, so it is highly likely that he was influenced by the ballad, as was Emily Brontë, in all probability, a century later.

"The Demon Lover" is used in this study to establish the plot formula which informs the literature under discussion. The ballad, it seems, directly or indirectly influenced Richardson as well as other fiction writers who use the seduction motif as a structural device to explore aggressor/victim interactions through their fiction. The ballad simplifies the demon-lover conflict in such a way that the underlying plot structure in more complex works of fiction may be illuminated by comparison to the more skeletal prototype. There is no single definitive ballad text for any given ballad, including "The Demon Lover." Consequently, chapter 3 examines fourteen representative texts in "The Demon Lover" complex in order to establish the core characteristics of the destructive conflict reflected by the demon-lover tales. The primary characteristic shared by the ballad and the demon-lover tales is the victimization of a woman by a man, a demon-lover figure who deliberately, wantonly degrades and destroys her.

Chapter 4 explores the dynamics involved in the highly destructive aggressor/victim conflict as it occurs in certain relationships between male and female characters in both nineteenth- and twentieth-century British fiction. The anatomy of the demon-lover conflict is of course expressed idiosyncratically by each author, but all of the authors whose work is discussed utilize the basic plot formula to convey meaning. Following an analysis of the ballad complex in chapter 3, an analysis which leads to the identification of a synthesized variant with its characteristic elements, selected works of fiction are interpreted in light of their similarity to the ballad.

Probably the most famous demon-lover of all time is Count Dracula. Relying on exotic legends and myths that comprise the demon-lover archetype, Bram Stoker tapped the collective unconscious when he created his bloodthirsty demonic lover. The connection between eroticism and death is best represented in *Dracula*, for a vampire's characteristic bite on the victim's neck means the kiss of death. The vampire legends which, in literature, culminate with *Dracula* provide richness and clarification regarding the sexual overtones inherent in demon-lover tales as well as the close psychic affinity between sexuality and violence. Female victims are both inexplicably attracted to and repelled by Dracula; they disregard their intuition concerning their own best interests, and instead obey the commands of the dangerous, foul-smelling, life-crushing Count Dracula. This dual response to the demon-lover figure is typical in the ballad and in all literature of this type. Beginning with the victim in the ballad, the women in these stories tend not to heed their own apprehensions, in favor of temptations offered by their demon-lovers. Victims often rush entranced toward their demise as they acquiesce to the commands of their demon-destroyers, who trick them into submission. As the dangerous figures in these works typically are dark, handsome, and appealing, women are physically drawn to them despite unmistakable clues revealing their pernicious temperaments.

The British Gothic tradition provides a way of examining the psychological contents of the pursuit narrative, as Gothic fiction involves a villain and a victim, dangerous landscapes, forbidding castles and mansions, abductions in the night, and so forth, all compatible with the demon-lover motif. Gothics are sexually charged works of psychological fiction which depend for their effect upon their readers' sense of fascination combined with moral outrage at the victimization that takes place. This dual impact on readers also distinguishes demon-lover tales from other works of fiction. Authors create demon-lover dramas according to their visions of obsessive love and violence. Each author deviates in some way from the ballad's plot formula, but the underlying structure of the conflict situation is remarkably similar from story to story. In chapter 4, these similarities and deviations are explored.

As a whole, then, this study is both historical and analytical. The demon-lover figure is traced through history and explored in several influential works of British fiction. A phenomenon as ancient and contemporary as the demon-lover conflict seems to be in the human consciousness needs, however, to be explained as well as analyzed. Some theorists would say that human aggression is a natural and desirable feature of being alive and that it is closely tied to survival. Others would say that aggression and hostility turned against others is an aberrant form of self-protectiveness; still others would view active aggression as a sign of moral collapse. The works of literature discussed here, among the most widely read of all time, reflect deliberate, aggressive acts perpetrated against victims who are essentially innocent. These works also, of course, demonstrate various views of victimization of women at the hands of vicious, unprincipled suitors. Relationships between lovers depend on trust, respect, and love, which means that all demon-lover tales convey a perversion of intimacy, a debauchery of love. Chapter 5 provides a psy-

choanalytic look at both players in the tragic drama and identifies the psychological dynamics that occur between ag-
gressor and victim. In that chapter, Jung's concepts of the
*animus* and *anima*, the "shadow" archetype, and projection
provide a theoretical framework for discussing the ballad and
the plot formula adapted by various fiction writers. Other
theorists, both well-accepted and controversial, provide tentative explanations for the highly volatile, reciprocal conflict
between victim and victimizer.

# TWO

## Demons as Lovers

Thou shalt not be afraid for the terror by night;
nor for the arrow that flieth by day;
Nor for the pestilence that walketh in darkness;
nor for the destruction that wasteth at noonday.

PSALM 91

Demons and the possibility of seduction and defilement at
their hands have always fascinated people. When Rubens
painted his *Rape of Europa*, for example, he captured a mythical
moment, a tableau dramatizing Zeus's seduction of Europa.
Taking the form of a bull, Zeus carries Europa off to Crete
against her will. The seduction motifs found in art and music
(e.g., Mozart's *Don Giovanni*) have their counterparts in literature. We have an early biblical example in the demon who
seduced Eve in the Garden of Eden. Stories about demons
are part of our cultural heritage and are represented through
the various arts but, more important, they are part of our
psychic makeup or, as Jung would say, part of our "collective
unconscious." In general, stories about demons who seduce
women are about power and powerlessness, will and sug-
gestibility, aggression and victimization.

One of the major expressions of the seduction motif is
found in "The Demon Lover," a Scottish border ballad that
has been in wide circulation since at least the seventeenth
century. The ballad, in fact, migrated to America at the end
of the eighteenth century and is currently one of the more
popular folk songs in this country. As the ballad's plot formula
closely resembles plot structures in works by Emily Brontë,
Thomas Hardy, D.H. Lawrence, Elizabeth Bowen, and oth-

ers, it is possible that these novelists were indirectly influenced by variations of "The Demon Lover." A close look at structural similarities will provide a means of assessing the influence of the ballad on these authors.

In the ballad complex known as "The Demon Lover" (Child 243; see Appendices), an aggressive male—the demon-lover—is presented as powerful, mysterious, supernatural, cruel, and obsessed, while the victim—always a woman in the ballad—is presented as vulnerable, malleable, and easily seduced and led astray. Many versions of the ballad have certain elements in common: a woman and her lover exchange secret vows; they separate for several years; the lover returns to claim the woman and then carries her off to her imminent destruction. The earliest known version of the ballad, Child A (see Appendix A), presents the demon-lover figure as a spirit, whereas in later versions (Child E, F, G) he has cloven feet, suggesting the Devil himself. In a number of variants, the demon-lover comes at night to his victim's window to persuade her to go away with him. Some versions of the ballad mention a vow, usually "a solemn vow," exchanged in the past between the lover and the victim, and often the lover tells the woman that he intends to punish her for breaking her vow to him—that is, for marrying someone else.

American variants in general tend to be less supernatural and more down-to-earth than their British predecessors, and the demon-lovers usually appear in more human form. The demon-lover in almost all of the British versions tempts the woman with promises of gold, while American versions usually substitute flashy items of clothing in order to emphasize her newfound wealth. For example, in an American variant entitled "The House Carpenter," collected by Arthur K. Davis, Jr., the woman "dressed herself in rich attire," and as she accompanies her demon-lover to his ship, "She shone like the glittering gold" (see Appendix B, version A). Another version tells us the woman "shined and she glittered and she boldly walked / The streets of Purity" (version B).

Both British and American versions show us women who are persuaded by vengeful lovers from their past to leave their homes and their families and to travel to unknown places. British versions, which more closely approximate the earliest known text of the border ballad, involve not only temptation in the form of gold and other riches but also travel to a foreign land, usually Italy. American versions, on the other hand, are adapted to include plot details that seem more in keeping with what might, when sung, sound like local geography; thus, ballads tend to gain geocentric details in place of exotic ones. For instance, the demon-lover in a Virginia text (Appendix B, version A) promises the woman a voyage to "the banks of the Sweet Willie," which seems clearly a corruption of the phrase "the banks of Italy," as most of the British versions read. As a result, the British ballad seems not only more supernatural, with spirits and demons for lovers, but also perhaps more exotic, as compared to American versions, which seem more domesticated.

In several versions, the vengeful lovers apparently grow to enormous size, as suggested by the way in which these lovers sink their ships, drowning the women they have tempted aboard. Typical of this size-changing or shape-shifting is the Child ballad version F, one of the more popular versions: "He strack the tap-mast wi his hand, / The fore-mast wi his knee, / And he brake that gallant ship in twain, / And sank her in the sea" (*The English and Scottish Popular Ballads*, p. 368). The supernatural shape-changing enables the demon-lover to destroy the ship, thereby accomplishing his revenge.

The title of the ballad, "The Demon Lover," combined with themes of revenge, temptation, shape-changing, and destruction strongly imply that we are indeed to see the lover as a demon who, like the prototypical Satan, brings chaos and death to the innocent or naive. In this case, the lover, a demon, woos his victim by telling her that he has sacrificed a great deal to return to her; then he promises her gold and persuades her to "sin" against her husband and children by abandoning them. The ballad comes from a long tradition of seduction tragedies; our responses to works of literature that repeat its plot formula depend upon historical and psychic associations we make regarding a determined lover's ability to seduce a woman, to woo her into submission, and thereby, often, to destroy her. Throughtout literary history the act of seduction has been repeatedly portrayed. Greek mythology provides excellent examples of mythical figures who are known for their propensity for seduction and terror. Hermes, son of Zeus, is a Greek fertility god often identified by his emblem, a phallus. Because he tricked Apollo, he is known for his deceit, but when they reconciled their differences Apollo gave Hermes a whip, symbolizing power and domination over others.[2] In Greek mythology it is Hermes who accompanies departed souls to Hades. Connections between seduction and alienation and between temptation and destruction are suggested by the idea of Hades, the underworld of the dead.

Hermes' son is Pan, a fertility demigod with the horns, ears, and legs of a goat. He is known as an amorous deity who chases and seduces goddesses, including Echo, Syrinx, and Selene. Like most Greek demigods, Pan is an ambiguous figure: in his pastoral setting he is a free-spirited and playful satyr, and yet he has a sinister side as well, which led to his being identified with Satan.

Silenus, son of Pan (or perhaps Hermes) is considered the leader of lustful satyrs and is associated with wine, drunkenness, and fertility. In Greek mythology—a primary source of the Judeo–Christian iconographical tradition—we may trace the development of the concept of Satan through, the offspring of Zeus; the lustfulness, the decadence, the destructiveness, and the goatlike appearance, especially the cloven hooves, came to be associated with the Devil.

The most important figure from Greek mythology for the present study is undoubtedly Pan because of his subsequent identification with Satan, for many Christians the archetypal image of evil. Regarding Pan's influence on the present image of Satan, Jeffrey Burton Russell states:

The iconographic influence of Pan upon the Devil is enormous. What in the tradition made it possible for the image of Pan to be joined with that of Satan? Medieval tradition frequently speaks of the hairiness of the Devil, sometimes of his horns, and occasionally of his cloven feet. The Devil is frequently described as taking animal forms, commonly that of the goat. The root of the similarity is the association of the Devil with the chthonic fertility deities, who were rejected by the Christians as demons along with the other pagan gods and who were particularly feared because of their association with the wilderness and with sexual frenzy. [*The Devil*, p. 126]

The connection between sexuality and the implicit danger of the wilderness (as represented by animal forms, specifically the goat) anticipates the theme of sexual passion which occurs in the wilderness, unacknowledged and uncondoned by society, as depicted in certain works of literature to be discussed in chapters 4 and 5.

Russell goes on to explain a conflict regarding sexuality that arose among Christians, a conflict born of the similarity between sexual ecstasy and death. This association of sexuality with death becomes central to an understanding of Satan as demonic antagonist and pursuer of women. According to Russell, "Sexual passion, which suspends reason and easily leads to excess, was alien both to the rationalism of the Greeks and to the asceticism of the Christians; a god of sexuality could easily be assimilated to the principle of evil. The association of the chthonic with both sex and the underworld, and hence with death, sealed the union" (p. 126). This conflict explains in part the fascination as well as the terror involved in destructive demon-lover encounters depicted in the literature to be discussed.

Through their fertility gods, the early Greeks began to associate sexuality with death, an association inherited by early Christians. When the ancients worshipped Hermes and Pan, they were, in a sense, worshipping the historical ancestors of Satan. A powerful mythological figure, similar in some ways to his Greek predecessors and associated with both sex and death, Satan is for Christians the embodiment of seduction, temptation, and evil. Prior to the figure of Satan which emerges by the end of the Old Testament period, other mythological figures were known as suitors who routinely harmed or destroyed the women they tempted or wooed, but Satan became the prototypical demon in pursuit of the innocent or naive.

Many classical scholars believe that mythological figures are metaphoric representations of human attitudes, hopes, fears, and conflicts. If they are, then perhaps they are equivalent to what psychologists today would call projections of the human psyche. Jung wrote, "all mythical figures correspond to inner psychic experiences and originally sprang from them" (*Four Archetypes*, p. 136), suggesting that mythical figures are the products of our vast psychic storehouse of images that we project onto our external world in order to understand our interior worlds better. In Jung's terms, Pan and later Satan, as well as his vast legion of demons, are images conjured up by the collective unconscious as a means of projecting evil.

In biblical times, belief in evil spirits or demons was widespread. But for the early Israelites, evil as well as good was sent by Yahweh or by his messengers or angels, called *mal'ākîm* (Barnett, "Satan," p. 752). Hebrews believed in a God who unified concepts of reward and punishment, good and evil. The concept of Satan as the personification of evil developed over time. Most biblical scholars agree that the word *satan* means "to persecute," "to be hostile to," "to pursue." Rivkah Schärf Kluger points out that while the verb *śātan*, appears only five times in the Old Testament, only in the Psalms, a secondary form of the verb, *śātam*, an apparently older form meaning "to entrap," appears in five Old Testament passages: once in Psalms, once in Job, and three times in Genesis (*Satan in the Old Testament*, pp. 26-27). The noun *śātān*, according to Kluger, "belonged originally to the profane sphere" (p. 32), as seen specifically in Arabic writings, and thus the noun is the original form from which the verbs were derived. The verb *śātan* implies inner opposition, she informs us, while the noun implies a mythological figure capable of willful destructiveness. As Kluger points out (p. 39), the only passage in the Old Testament where the word *satan* has an article indicating a proper name is the most recent one, 1 Chronicles, 21:1. The concept of Satan in the Old Testament, then, evolved from an abstract idea regarding punishment and opposition to a personification of evil.[3]

By the time the New Testament was written, beliefs about Satan had, predictably, changed. It is clear from Luke (chapters 10 and 18) and the Apocalypse (12:7-9) that instead of explaining evil as a manifestation of Yahweh's desire to punish, many people of that era believed that, sometime in the past, Satan had fallen from his divine position as God's messenger. Whereas in the Old Testament Satan was considered an enforcer of higher laws, he is seen in the New Testament as the *source* of temptation, destruction, disease, and evil. In the New Testament he is referred to most often as Satan or the Devil (*diabolos* is a translation of the Hebrew word *satan*), but he is also called "Beelzeboul," "the enemy," "the evil one," "the prince of demons," and other names (Russell, pp. 228-29).

Christians have always attributed a great deal of power to Satan. Stories regarding Satan's ability to corrupt people, to tempt them into rejecting the Christian faith in favor of the demonic ideal of destruction, circulated widely during the early Middle Ages. Pictures of Satan, hell, and the Last Judgment were painted on the walls of churches during the twelfth century (Cavendish, *The Powers of Evil*, p. 208), thereby impressing on people's minds graphic images of the Devil. "The Devil who presides over these infernos," writes Cavendist, "is sometimes a human figure with a certain dignity, but more often he is a hideous monster whose ugliness shows his spiritual corruption" (p. 208). The idea that the Devil may appear in the form of a human being as well as a monstrous chthonic figure is critical to the medieval concept of demonology: Satan, it was thought, takes whatever form necessary to seduce, persuade, or trick people into serving him.

The witches[4] and the witchcraft trials which occurred from the eleventh century to the late seventeenth century testify to the widespread belief in Satan's ability to form small bands of converts dedicated to destructiveness. Several secular magistrates—Henri Boguet, Pierre de Lancre, Nicolas Remy, and others—who presided over the witchcraft trials in England wrote highly influential books in which they recorded numerous cases of alleged witchcraft, often relating exactly how Satan tempted the accused (usually women) into serving him.[5] Remy's *Demonolatry* is especially helpful for understanding not so much what actually happened as what people *thought* was true about witches. Remy, who served as magistrate in Lorraine for sixteen years, during which more than eight hundred "witches" were charged, pronounced guilty, and condemned to death (p. 56), reveals what seems like authoritative commentary on the interactions between Satan and the women whom he had won through devious means. Remy establishes the steps by which Satan snares both willing and unwilling devotees. According to Remy and other writers of that period, Satan is able to take whatever form is most effective. To create a sense of confidence, for example, he may assume the guise of a prosperous merchant and at the same time conceal all indications that he is evil or deceptive (p. 32); or he may wear a long black cloak associated with upstanding citizens in order to give his words more authority (p. 69).

As Remy explains it, nearly all of the women who confessed to the crime of witchcraft in Lorraine stated that the Devil visited them at night in the form of a cat or a mouse who came in through the window. The Devil assumes whatever shape will be convincing, then lures his victim by means of certain promises: if the woman seeks revenge, Satan provides the opportunity to achieve it; if the woman seeks riches, Satan plays on her greed, offering "a false display of riches" (p. 1). The theme of false riches is consistently mentioned in the literature on demonology. Gold, or sometimes silver, is used to tempt victims into servitude. The gold, however, almost always dissolves into dust once the women are under Satan's control, just as in the ballad the gold dissolves once the victim is aboard ship and under the demon-lover's control.

In appearance, Satan is usually black, a color often associated with deception, with the supernatural, with night, and with death. John Rodker, editor of the 1930 edition of Remy's *Demonolatry*, provides a gloss regarding Satan's appearance as reported by several "witches" who had confessed to the crime of witchcraft during the sixteenth and seventeenth centuries. Rodker relates the following reports of initial meetings with the Devil:

> John Walsh of Dorsetshire, 1566, described the Devil as "Sometymes like a man in all proportions, sauing that he had clouen feete." Margaret Johnson, one of the Lancashire coven in 1633, stated that there appeared to her "a spirit or divell in the similitude and proportion of a man, apparelled in a suite of black, tyed about wth silke pointes." A Yarmouth witch in 1644 "heard one knock at her Door, and rising to her Window, she saw, it being Moonlight, a tall black Man there." Joan Wallis of Keiston in Huntingdonshire said that "the Devill came to her in the likenesse of a man in blackish cloathing, but had cloven feet." Susanna Edwards, a Devonshire witch, 1682, said: "She did meet with a gentlemen in a field called the Parsonage Close in the town of Biddiford. And saith that his apparrel was all of black. . . . [ellipsis Rodker's]. Being demanded what and who the gentleman she spake of was, the said examinant answered and said, That it was the Devil." At the famous North Berwick meeting in 1590 the Devil "was clad in ane blak gown with ane blak hat upon his head." (p. 69)

In addition to presenting the recurring image of the Devil as a man dressed in black clothing who often has cloven feet, Rodker's citations emphasize that Satan pursues people at night in the relative safety of their own homes and neighborhoods. Once under Satan's control these "witches" accompanied him into the wilderness or into the woods where they were away from society, very much as the victim in the ballad is lured away from her familiar surroundings.

A connection between Satan and sexuality has been widely accepted. One of the central activities that supposedly took

place during witches' sabbats was sexual adoration of the demon figure, including—but not limited to—sexual intercourse. In his study Remy writes, "And all female witches
maintain that the so-called genital organs of their Demons are
so huge and so excessively rigid that they cannot be admitted
without the greatest pain" (p. 14). Identifying Satan and other
demons with sexuality, especially with huge phalluses, may
very well trace back to Greek mythology. The connection between sex and pain or cruelty seems unmistakably related to
an urge to destroy: rather than being a creative or procreative
event, sexual union becomes a means of expressing hatred
and evil. The supposed pact between Satan and so-called
witches is, in a sense, a demon-lover arrangement whereby
suggestible women are tempted by certain promises to com-
promise their will and are persuaded to embark on a course
of self-destruction.

For centuries it has been thought that not only Satan but
also demons of lesser power are compelled to tempt women
and to lead them into submission. Early Jews and Christians
came to believe that Satan ruled over a legion of demons.
Originally, the concept of demons had pagan connotations
which were incorporated into the Old Testament. For example, many of the demons that populate the desert in Isaiah
resemble Pan, and, in fact, many of them are called śe'īrîm
(or śēdîm) from the Hebrew word śā'îr, meaning "the hairy
one, the he-goat," a word often translated in English as "satyrs" (Kluger, p. 44).

In the Septuagint, good spirits are referred to as angels and
evil spirits are called demons; the demons, however, were
thought to be instruments of Yahweh and as a group they
were subservient to the satan of 1 Chronicles. Placing the demons of the Old Testament in historical perspective, Russell
contends, "The demons, then, were in part personifications
of the evil attributes previously associated with the gods. They
also acquired some of the characteristics previously ascribed
to monsters, characteristics that passed on in iconography and
legend to the Devil himself" (p. 70). In the New Testament,
names of demons occur frequently, especially in the Gospels.

The most frequent names of demons are: *daimonion, daimon, archai, exousiai, dynameis, kuriotetes, thronoi, onomata, archontes, kyrioi, theoi, stoicheia,* and *angeloi* (Russell, p. 236). Satan and his demons were thought to be fallen angels who were eternally damned and separated from God; thus, Christian tradition further removed them from the divine associations found in early Hebrew scripture.

During the Middle Ages and the Renaissance, religious leaders attempted to identify and list all of the evil spirits. Consequently, hierarchies of demons were established as well as classification systems intended to identify types of evil influences. One of the more influential works on this subject was King James's *Daemonologie* (1597) in which evil spirits are divided into four main categories. The first type, those he calls *Lemures* or *Spectra*, are the most common evil spirits and haunt houses and solitary places. The second type, *umbrae mortuorum*, are spirits of the dead and generally annoy people; these spirits are often referred to as incubi and succubi. The third category of evil spirits includes demons or spirits that occupy a person's body and possess him. The fourth type, not as evil as the others, are called *spirites* or *Pharies* (de Bruyn, *Woman & the Devil*, p. 112). Commenting on the serious effort on the part of medieval thinkers to identify Satan's legion of demons, Cavendish reports, "Estimates varied, but according to some authorities there were originally 399,920,004 angels altogether, so that the total of fallen angels was 133,306,668" (p. 234). Clearly, concern with demons was uppermost in the minds of many people during the Middle Ages and Renaissance.

Fear of demons was inherited from the Greeks, who believed in spirits, both good and evil. Demons of the underworld or of the sea were called Gorgons; another type of demon, called Keres, Russell describes as "ghosts who could be benign but who were more likely to cause nightmares, blindness, or madness. The Keres had gnashing fangs and blue-black, horrible faces; they drank the blood of the dying" (pp. 142-43). In the same way that pagan Greeks believed in Keres and Gorgons, citizens of medieval England and Scotland believed in similar spirits; dwarves, trolls, fairies, elves, kobolds, gnomes, leprechauns, and demons called "green men," "wild men," or "men of the forest" were all part of the folklore of the age. As Cavendish suggests, at some point these popular folk figures became "demonized" (p. 187). Many people thought that the less powerful demons, such as elves and kobolds, became *familiars* for witches, demons who personally attached themselves to witches in order to offer their guidance and influence.

During the Middle Ages many people believed in incubi and succubi that visited people during the night for the purpose of sexual intercourse. An incubus was believed to be a demon that assumed the form of a man; a succubus assumed a female form. According to Cavendish, these demons materialized as a result of "either animating a corpse for the purpose of manufacturing a body from condensed air or smoke, or from male sperm ejaculated in masturbation or nocturnal emission" (p. 103).

He goes on to explain that Thomas Aquinas thought that with a man, a demon would take the form of a succubus in order to acquire the sperm necessary to impregnate a woman once the demon took the form of an incubus (p. 102). Whether offspring was possible from such a mating was debated during the Middle Ages, but certainly folklore of the day was rich with stories of "demonic" children.

In the Middle Ages, many people believed that nightmares were actually evil spirits that came in the night to frighten or suffocate the sleeper. In Latin, the word "nightmare" is *incubo* (Cavendish, p. 102), so the association is understandable. Stith Thompson discusses several folktales popular in England and Europe during this period that feature the Nightmare or Alp, a spirit that strangles or suffocates people in their sleep, as well as the Incubus, an evil spirit who seduces women as they sleep (*The Folktale*, p. 249). Connections among sleep (a deathlike state), sexuality, and the demonic seem to have been extremely strong during this period in history. In fact, many accused witches claim to have experienced sexual intercourse with spirits and demons while asleep, and in several folktales, the devil comes to people in the form of death (p. 45).

In "The Demon Lover," the revenant lover usually comes to the woman's house at night, often to the window, to persuade her to go away with him. At the time the ballad first circulated in Scotland and England, people no doubt were reminded of stories similar to those recorded by Nicolas Remy and the other magistrates describing initial contact with the Devil. In many versions of the ballad, some of the oldest versions in fact, the lover takes the form of a spirit. Scottish folklore is replete with tales and legends of spirits, demons, and other supernatural beings that could very well have influenced the anonymous balladeer who composed the earliest version of the ballad later known as "The Demon Lover." A kelpie for example was, hundreds of years ago and still today, believed to be a water spirit that usually takes the form of a horse that destroys and drowns his unwary victims. At times, the kelpie takes the shape of a man who first has sexual intercourse with his female victim before drowning her (Cavendish, pp. 245-46). The Scots also believed in the existence of the *baobhan sith*, vampire fairies that visit people during the night and are similar to the liliths, lamias, striges, and estries of continental Europe (p. 242). The Nuckelavee, which supposedly haunts the Lowlands of Scotland, is a hideous half-man, half-horse demon, hairless and skinless, which terrorizes people because it hates humankind (p. 230).

Because the demon-lover in the ballad is called a "spirit" in some versions, a question arises regarding the corporeality of the returning lover. That the dead can return as spirits to menace the living is suggested by the words of the song. Plato once stated that a man who overly attaches himself to worldly concerns and material existence cannot sever his ties to earth after death; hence, he is bound to haunt the earth, occasionally possessing and tormenting the living. During the Reformation, Protestants raised the issue of ghosts by challenging the Catholic belief in purgatory. Medieval and Renaissance literature, and the Gothic literature of the eighteenth and nineteenth centuries, is filled with dead persons who return to haunt the living. The enormous popularity of vampire stories during the nineteenth century testifies to the widespread belief and interest in ghosts, especially those who ravish women. Today, many occultists believe that ghosts are caused by extreme emotional states *projected*—like a nightmare—into the astral realm.

Several versions of "The Demon Lover" involve a spirit who comes in the night or a demonic lover with cloven feet, suggesting supernatural abduction. When the ballad first circulated, people tended to be superstitious; they fully believed in the possibility of being carried off in the middle of the night by spirits, ghosts, or demons. At that time, the word "nightmare" meant an incubus or ghost who returns to his victim to carry her off during sleep, when her unconscious is vulnerable.

Ballads, especially the Child ballads, are the songs of the common people, and as such, they reflect the hopes and fears of the community in which they first circulated. Balladeers, in other words, interpreted the collective emotional environments in which they found themselves. Ballad scholars unanimously point to "The Demon Lover" as an example of a ballad that, despite corruptions of the text, has remained a favorite among contemporary ballad singers. Furthermore, many of the works of fiction that appear to utilize the ballad's plot formula have been immensely popular: *Wuthering Heights* and *Tess of the d'Urbervilles*, for example.

The repetition and popularity of the plot formula over the years raise several interesting questions. Is there something inherent in the plot that is universally recognizable? How do the two participants in the drama create personal and collective emotional responses in us? Does the fate of the victim correspond to personal and collective fears? Why are we fascinated by the violence perpetrated by demon-lover figures?

These questions will be addressed primarily in chapters 4 and 5, but before tentative answers to these questions are introduced, the structural and thematic similarities between the ballad and the literary works identified as demon-lover tales must be established. In chapter 3, a brief historical overview of ballad scholarship is provided, followed by an in-depth analysis of "The Demon Lover"; the core characteristics among variants are isolated; and a composite version of the ballad is presented, a version against which the literary works are later compared.

# THREE

## "The Demon Lover" Ballad

I love a ballad in print, a life,
for then we are sure they are true.

SHAKESPEARE,
*The Winter's Tale*

Many scholars believe that the ballad form originated during the Middle Ages. Long before that, however, there were myths, legends, tales, and other genres peculiar to folk cultures that no doubt provided various themes and stories later adopted by balladeers. As M.J. Hodgart and others inform us, folklore apparently traveled along the trade routes of Europe (*The Ballads*, p. 84), resulting in a cross-cultural exchange of folkloric traditions. Consequently, British folktales, ballads, and other forms often resemble older European and Scandinavian versions; in the same way, those found in America often have British roots.[6]

Many ballad scholars believe that the Scottish border region was the center of ballad life during the Middle Ages and the Renaissance; Hodgart and others point out that Aberdeenshire in particular was among the more prolific areas for ballads. It is interesting that, of all the ballads circulating in Britain, those indigenous to Aberdeenshire are most similar to supernatural Scandinavian versions (Hodgart, p. 85, quoting Alexander Keith). This commonality suggests, perhaps, constant trade by the people of Aberdeenshire with Scandinavian mariners who traveled back and forth across the English Channel, bringing folk beliefs, folktales, and ballads back with them.

Evelyn Kendrick Wells, among other scholars, believes that

the border region was an ideal location for ballad-making due to its rugged, wild topography, its history of vengeance and violence, its clan-centered social economy, and its strong poetic tradition. The local feuds and the frequent raids along the border provided a very colorful backdrop for ballad stories. Regarding the border region, Wells remarks that "there runs through all the history, literature, and oral tradition of the Border a continuous sombre note of treachery, murder, cruelty, barbarity—and romantic loyalty" (*The Ballad Tree*, p. 58). Along the border, vengeance precipitated by family vendettas played a major role in social interactions. Wells notes, for example, that the right hand of a male child was sometimes left unbaptized to enable him to seek vengeance against his clan's enemies (p. 62).

Due to widespread diffusion, determining the geographic origin of a single ballad is often impossible. Definitively dating a ballad is also nearly impossible, because countless versions circulated for years before a version was first written down or printed. The versions we have in manuscript form may or may not have been the most popular or the best examples that ever circulated.[7] One way of tentatively dating a ballad, though, is to identify the earliest manuscript or text in which the ballad first appears. Child prints only six ballads found in manuscripts older than the year 1500. The oldest extant ballad text, "Judas" (Child 23), appears in a thirteenth-century manuscript.

Before the invention of printing, some ballads were copied by hand and collected in manuscript form. But once cheap printing became available in the sixteenth century, street hawkers began to sell broadside ballads to a public that eagerly read them. During the sixteenth and seventeenth centuries a number of folk ballads currently circulating were written down and distributed as broadside sheets which specified the tunes to which the songs should be sung. The earliest known broadside version of "The Demon Lover," for example, was to be sung "To a West-country tune called 'The Fair Maid of Bristol,' 'Bateman,' or 'John True,' " (Child, p. 360).[8] Many broadsides were composed for the immediate profit they would bring; thus, they were usually hackneyed, though dramatic enough to please their buyers, who especially relished plots that told of murder, revenge, and romantic tragedy. Successful ballads were those that reflected the beliefs of the people and were easily assimilated, making the professional balladists, as Albert B. Friedman puts it, "merely deputies of the public voice" (*The Ballad Revival*, p. 61).

Despite legislation prohibiting the distribution of ballads in the sixteenth century, broadsides were extremely popular.[9] But by the end of the seventeenth century, according to Friedman, the broadside ballad industry began to decline, precipitating what he calls "the ballad revival," a term used to signify efforts to collect and study ballads. One of the most famous collections of the popular Black-Letter ballads is that of Samuel Pepys. His collection, completed in 1703,[10] preserves over sixteen hundred ballads, including the oldest known version of "The Demon Lover," a broadside then known by the long title "A Warning for Married Women, being an example of Mrs. Jane Reynolds (a West-country woman), born near Plymouth, who, having plighted her troth to a Seaman, was afterwards married to a Carpenter, and at last carried away by a Spirit, the manner how shall presently be recited" (Child, p. 360). Percy and later collectors and scholars have criticized Pepys for tampering with ballad texts and for compiling broadsides with questionable literary merit. Pepys does, however, provide the earliest known versions of many ballads, which makes his collection invaluable.

During the eighteenth century, printed chapbooks, containing broadsides and often jokes, stories, sermons, and other material, became immensely popular with the common people. Chapbooks were widely sought after by poor people, who, over the years, formed inexpensive collections of folk literature. Many ballads began to appear in songbooks; thus, certain ballads circulated simultaneously in oral tradition and in printed versions via street hawkers and published books. Allan Ramsay's *The Ever Green* (1724) and *The Tea-Table Miscellany* (1723-1737), the anonymously edited *A Collection of Old*

*Ballads* (1723-1725), as well as David Herd's *Ancient and Modern Scottish Songs* (1756) and *Ancient and Modern Scots Songs* (1769), consisting mainly of broadsides, helped to circulate ballads that would not otherwise have been so widely disseminated. Both Sir Walter Scott and Francis James Child later relied on Herd's ballad books for their own highly influential works.

But it was Thomas Percy's *Reliques of Ancient Poetry* (1765) that did more than any other work to promote interest in the ballad and which is therefore considered the first important ballad collection, containing a number of ballads dating from about 1560 (Hodgart, p. 72). Friedman calls *Reliques* "the pivotal document of the ballad revival" (p. 185). Percy used Pepys's earlier collection as a major source of broadsides, and since many of Percy's ballads are contained in Child's *The English and Scottish Popular Ballads*, Percy can be seen as a pivotal figure whose work bridges almost two hundred years of ballad collecting. Percy is also known as the first person to use the word "ballad" to mean popular narrative poetry (Hodgart, p. 78), a word made popular by the literary balladists of the pre-Romantic and Romantic periods, who relied on Percy's work for inspiration (G. Malcolm Laws, *British Literary Ballad*, p. 5).

Scott's *Minstrelsy of the Scottish Border* (1802-1803) is considered another important ballad book because of the polished, readable condition of the ballads. We know now, however, that Scott presented composite versions and that he embellished and "improved" quite a number of the ballads in his collection, as did several of his predecessors. But *Minstrelsy* was highly popular and promoted widespread interest in the ballad form. In Scott's work "The Demon Lover" first appeared under that title, a title by which many subsequent versions are known, including many American texts. In his headnote, Scott remarks that the ballad "contains a legend, which, in various shapes, is current in Scotland" (p. 246).

Scott's version of "The Demon Lover" is collected in Child's volume as well as the version included in the next important ballad collection, William Motherwell's *Minstrelsy, Ancient and Modern* (1827). Motherwell supported the idea that ballad texts should not be tampered with. Friedman, quoting from Motherwell's "Introduction," writes, " 'The tear and wear of three centuries will do less mischief to the text of an old ballad among the vulgar, than one short hour will effect, if in the possession of some . . . editor of the present day, who cuts and trims and embellishes his texts with 'tailor-like fastidiousness' " (pp. 245-46). Scott's view represents an attitude about ballads that was by then about two hundred years old: ballads are too vulgar to be read by the general public and must be touched up and made presentable. On the other hand, Motherwell, thinking perhaps of Scott's work when he made his remark, represents a growing sentiment that ballads should be preserved exactly as they are sung by the folk in a condition as close as possible to their original versions.

Despite much concern among present-day scholars about tampering with ballads by editors, it is nevertheless true that once a new version is printed, it enters folk culture and alters the history of that ballad forever. The popularity of songbooks and ballad collections—those with "authentic" versions and those with "corrupt" versions—undoubtedly perpetuated ballads that would otherwise have faded into obscurity. As printed versions of particular ballads gained popularity, the oral tradition was often supplanted by the printed versions, especially in the cities where broadsides were more readily available. Some ballad scholars believe that broadsides truncated the lives of ballads, while others believe that the broadside tradition is precisely what has preserved a great many ballads that would otherwise have been lost. It is probably more accurate to say that oral and written versions acted on one another, resulting in versions that acquired characteristics of both. Referring to remarks made by Gordon Hall Gerould and others, Friedman points out that "it has been noted by ballad scholars that matter learned from print rather than by ear strongly resists alteration" (p. 62). Friedman goes on to suggest, however, that due to the enormous output of broadsides the natural course of ballad evolution that normally occurred in oral tradition was interfered with. Printed versions of ballads vary from songbook to songbook, suggesting that the evolution of printed forms follows the same general pattern as versions in oral tradition; that is, changes occur depending on the particular preferences of editors as well as singers.

Widely recognized as a monumental piece of scholarship, Child's *The English and Scottish Popular Ballads* (1882-1898) includes over a thousand versions of the 305 ballads in the collection, including numerous broadsides. These ballads have since been referred to as traditional ballads or Child ballads. As Child left no formal definition of what he called "the popular ballad," other scholars have attempted to identify the criteria he used in his collection and have formulated various working definitions. Gerould provides an excellent general definition of a Child ballad when he states, "A ballad is a folksong that tells a story with stress on the crucial situation, tells it by letting the action unfold itself in event and speech, and tells it objectively with little comment or intrusion of personal bias" (*The Ballad of Tradition*, p. 11). Hodgart describes the Child ballads as a group in the following way:

They are anonymous, narrative poems, nearly always written down in short stanzas of two or four lines. They are distinguished from all other types of narrative poetry by a peculiar and effective way of telling their stories. They deal with one single situation and deal with it dramatically, beginning "in the fifth act"; and there is a high proportion of dialogue to stage-direction. They are not only anonymous but also impersonal: the story-teller does not intrude his personality, and there is no moralizing or didacticism. Again, the ballads are distinguished from all other types of poetry by their complete freedom from the poetic diction fashionable in any period: they have their own peculiar rhetoric and phraseology. [pp. 10-11]

Among the border ballads and those from Aberdeenshire are a high proportion that reflect pagan notions of the supernatural, especially belief in magic spells, witches, demons, and revenant beings. G. Malcolm Laws reminds us that many people in the communities in which supernatural ballads circulated actually believed the superstitions, legends, and tales upon which many ballads are based. For example, the oldest version of "The Demon Lover," the one entitled "A Warning for Married Women," was recorded in Pepys's collection at a time when women (and men) were still being put to death for witchcraft.[11] Many people tried for witchcraft during the sixteenth century testified that human sacrifices were necessary every seven years. In four of the seven versions of ballad Child 243 (versions A, D, E, and F), the revenant lover had been away for seven years before returning to wreak vengeance on the woman to whom he had been betrothed. It is curious that seven years is also the interval after which a diabolical figure in the ballad returns to destroy a woman by supernatural means. The time element in the ballad and reports made by accused witches appear to be mutually reinforcing elements. The seven-year time lapse in the ballad remained stable for three centuries, from the seventeenth to the nineteenth.

In many ballads of the supernatural ("The Demon Lover," for example), a mysterious, otherworldly landscape is a significant feature. Entrance to the otherworld is often gained by way of trees, mountains, and caves, and in some ballads death by drowning initiates journeys by water to the other world (Wells, p. 138). In the ballads, the attitude toward the supernatural is matter-of-fact; the tone is objective, as stories of elves, witches, ghosts, and demons are told with what John Veitch calls "simple, unastonished realism" (quoted in Wells, p. 142). Commenting on an interest in the supernatural and on the evolutionary changes to supernatural ballads over time, Laws states:

That the folk who preserved the ballads about ghosts, fiends, witches, and revenants accepted them as literally true is abundantly clear. Those who have collected balladry from traditional singers have been impressed time and again by the fact that the singers wholeheartedly believe the stories they tell in song. Furthermore, if some occurrence in an older ballad ceases to be credible, that ballad is likely to be either dropped from tradition or modified to eliminate the no longer meaningful details. Thus, the supernatural has tended to disappear from British traditional balladry in modern times, especially in America, where belief in the supernatural is less strong than in the British Isles. But where belief still exists, the supernatural ballad will be found. [*British Literary Ballad*, pp. 26-27]

In general, Scottish ballads deal more with the supernatural than do English ballads. Ballads that circulated in more than one country, such as "The Demon Lover," acquired characteristics particular to each country; thus, versions influenced by Scottish tradition tend to be more supernatural. The stories told in American versions of British ballads are the least supernatural of all, owing partly, perhaps, to a more "rational," less superstitious cultural heritage and partly to the predictable changes that ballads undergo over time.[12] Roger D. Abrahams and George Foss, in *Anglo-American Folksong Style*, theorize that if certain features appear ridiculous, offensive, or psychologically threatening, they are consciously or unconsciously rejected. References to incest, for instance, tend to disappear from more recent texts. According to many folklorists, magic and supernatural events dissipate rather easily, especially in ballads that are transported great distances. Ghosts, demons, and other folk characters become humanized, particularly when they circulate in more sophisticated society.

As ballad scholars point out, seldom can the seminal version of a ballad be identified. Initially Andrew Lang, then Francis B. Gummere and others, postulated that folk communities as a whole invented ballads and other folk songs that expressed something of importance to that community Gummere calls this act of ballad-making "communal re-creation." As songs were dispersed and transmitted from place to place and from generation to generation, they changed. By the time Pepys, Percy, Scott, and the others collected their ballads, they were collecting versions that undoubtedly differed significantly from the earliest ballads. Printed versions which came after the earliest broadside undoubtedly "contaminated" oral tradition in the same way that orally transmitted versions were written down in altered form. Printed and oral versions of any one ballad, then, have a shared and mutually influencing history. To support this point, one might examine the differences that took place in the hundred years or so between the time Pepys collected "A Warning for Married Women" and the time Scott collected "The Demon Lover."

Child A (see Appendix A), collected by Pepys in 1685 according to Child, consists of thirty-two stanzas, making it not only the oldest but also the longest known version in "The Demon Lover" complex. Scott's version (see Appendix C), published in 1802, has nineteen stanzas.[13] Because the earliest known version is a broadside, it is fixed in time, as compared to versions in oral tradition, which tend to be altered somewhat each time they are sung. Scott explains in his headnote to the ballad that his version was "taken down from recitation by Mr. William Laidlaw," who claims to have heard it from a Mr. Walter Grieve (p. 246). He further explains that Laidlaw "improved" the fragment presented by Grieve by adding three stanzas and repeating part of another.

There are several features of the Pepys version that are missing or altered in the later variation. Most apparent is the lack of preliminary details; while the earlier version devotes the first fifteen stanzas to setting the scene and providing motivating factors for the action to follow, the later version begins *in medias res* with a conversation between the two former lovers. With Scott's version, the conflict in the plot is immediate, whereas the earlier one builds to the conflict only after presenting detailed background information. But that information is important because through it we learn that the lover, James Harris, who has presumably just returned from sea, was killed "Within a forraign land" seven years earlier. Thus, by the time he comes to Jane Reynolds' window as "A spirit in the night," we begin to sense the extent of her danger. The preliminary stanzas appear only in the old broadside, as subsequent versions all begin with the conversation between the man and the woman regarding their vow of faithfulness. In the fourth stanza of the broadside we find out that in the past James Harris and Jane Reynolds had sworn an oath together: "And to each other secretly / They made a solemn vow." This element is retained in the Scott version as well as in most of the other British versions but is softened a bit, for when the demon-lover comes for his betrothed, he says to her, "O I'm come to seek my former vows, / Ye granted me before."

In the Scott version, the woman kisses her children goodbye, a feature of the plot introduced into print first by Scott and repeated in later collections. This addition to the plot provides pathos and makes the woman seem a little more reasonable than the woman in the broadside who simply flees with a spirit that no more than resembles a man. However, in Scott's version, once aboard ship the woman suddenly notices her companion's cloven feet, an act that has two important implications: first, it strongly suggests that the woman had been blinded in some way and was unaware of or oblivious to her surroundings, as if she had been in a trance; second, it implies a direct association with the Devil. Both Pepys's and Scott's versions deal with the supernatural, though in different ways, for over time the revenant lover had become a demon. The demon-lover with the cloven feet is the dominant feature of the ballad that circulated in the British Isles during the nineteenth century.[14] The title of the ballad, "The Demon Lover," as well as the motif of the revenant lover as demon-destroyer remains stable throughout the nineteenth century.

In Scott's version we also find the first mention of the mountains of heaven and hell, an image which reinforces a sense of evil foreboding in the ballad. Scott presents this image in two stanzas:

> "O what hills are yon, yon pleasant hills,
> That the sun shines sweetly on?"
> "O yon are the hills of heaven," he said,
> "Where you will never win."
>
> "O whaten a mountain is yon," she said,
> "All so dreary wi' frost and snow?"
> "O yon is the mountain of hell," he cried,
> "Where you and I will go." [*Minstrelsy*, p. 251]

These stanzas were usually consolidated into one stanza by succeeding British compilers, but the image consistently appeared in their versions.[15] The cloven-footed demon-lover along with visions of heaven and hell combine to create for the reader a mythopoetic encounter with evil. Significantly, Scott's is also the first text in which the demon murders the woman by sinking the ship using supernatural means. After Scott, the plot almost always ends with the woman drowning at the hands of her demon-lover. In only one prior version, Child B, from *The Rambler's Garland* (1785 [?]), does the woman drown, along with the mariner, but the cause of the disaster is not specified. In Scott's text, though, the demon-lover deliberately, wantonly destroys her.

In more than one hundred years between the two versions, the ballad had become less localized and historical, and more impersonal. The names James Harris and Jane Reynolds and the geographical location, "Neer unto Plimouth," were dropped. Preliminary information regarding the romantic history of the former lovers is also dropped; thus, no motivating factors are provided. Over time, the language became far less emotional; for example, in the earlier version, when the woman first sees the spirit at her window, she reacts with "sorely fright," whereas the woman in the later version reacts by asking him a friendly question: "O where have you been, my long, long love, / This long seven years and more?" The earlier version is the only surviving text in which the woman is said to love her former lover once he returns; in contrast, the woman in Scott's version weeps when she notices his cloven feet, thereby recognizing her dire predicament.[16] In the broadside, the carpenter hangs himself when he learns of his wife's death, leaving the children orphans; this element of the plot is eliminated in all subsequent versions, although in Child C (from Peter Buchan's *Ancient Ballads and Songs of the North of Scotland*, published in 1828) the carpenter laments for the final three stanzas.

Hodgart studies the migration of ballads by analyzing "Lord Thomas and Fair Annet" (Child 73), establishing what he calls "families" of the ballad. As with all ballads, there is no single, original version to point to as the one from which all other versions were derived. Hodgart, though, identifies five groups or families into which the "Lord Thomas" complex divides. His purpose is to identify not the original version but the originating ballad family or geographical location. In the same way, "The Demon Lover" complex can be divided into three families: English, Scottish, and American.[17]

Scholars John Burrison and Alisoun Gardner-Medwin agree that, on the basis of common dialects, images, and plot features, the English versions appear to be Child texts A and B, and Scottish texts appear to be C, D, E, and F (which is perhaps Irish), and the fragment G. Burrison contends that American versions have English roots, as the earliest American text, published by De Marsan in New York in 1860, resembles the two earliest known broadsides that circulated in England two hundred years before. The ballad, he surmises, must have been brought to this country by English and Scotch-Irish immigrants just prior to 1800. Gardner-Medwin, on the other hand, believes that the Scottish influence is even greater, even though many American versions are similar to Child B. Gardner-Medwin bases her case on certain plot elements shared only by Scottish and American variants; the most convincing feature that she points to is the mysterious promised land where the demon-lover offers to take his victim, changing from "the banks of Italy" in Child versions C, D, E, F, and G, to "the Sweet Willie," "the banks of old Tennessee," or to a place that similarly rhymes with "Italy." Gardner-Medwin concludes that Scottish emigrants brought the popular ballad to Pennsylvania and Virginia during the first half of the eighteenth century. It is likely that both researchers are correct and that several waves of immigration from Great Britain during the 1700s resulted in effective dissemination of the ballad.

American versions have been widely collected but are represented in this study by Arthur Kyle Davis, Jr., who presents twenty-seven variations in *Traditional Ballads of Virginia*. Texts collected by Davis are representative of American versions of "The Demon Lover" which in this country most resemble Child B, although a few include a heaven-and-hell stanza derived from Scott. The only names mentioned in the portion of the ballad complex represented in this study are James Harris and Jane Reynolds of the broadside, Jeanie Douglas and James Harris of Child C (Peter Buchan's), and Fair Ellen of Davis F and Q, probably an intrusion of a character's name from "Child Waters" (Child 62).

The accompanying table compares the Child variants of "The Demon Lover" as well as the first seven versions in Davis' anthology (versions which provide a representative sampling), by dividing the compiled ballad into various incidents. Together these incidents form what Hodgart calls a "montage," named after the filmmaking technique that joins " 'shots' or 'frames' together significantly" (p. 27). The three "families" of versions— English, Scottish, and American—are tabulated in Table 1 according to incidents represented by each family.

The table makes possible several relevant observations about the history of "The Demon Lover." Child A, a broadside dated 1685, is the oldest extant version; Child B, C, D, E, F, and G—later variations dated 1785, 1828, 1827, 1827, 1802-1803, and 1827, respectively—evolved either from the broad-

Table 1. Families of "The Demon Lover" Ballad

| Incident | Family | | |
| --- | --- | --- | --- |
| | English | Scottish | American |
| 1. A* & B exchanged secret vows in the past | Vows not secret in most versions; in some, no vow | Vows, but not secret | No vows |
| 2. A goes to sea before marriage | Only in broadside. Gone 7 years; in some, no mention of years | Gone 7 years | No mention |
| 3. News comes to B of A's death in a foreign land | Only in broadside | No | No |
| 4. C woos B | Only in broadside | No | No |
| 5. B and C marry | Mentioned in broadside. In most others, B tells A. Missing in the fragment G | B tells A | B tells A |
| 6. B and C have children | Three in broadside; one son in others | Two in one version; one son in the others | One child in all |
| 7. C goes on trip | Only in broadside | No | No |
| 8. Spirit of A comes to window | Only in broadside | No | No |
| 9. A persuades B to go away with him | Directly in some, implied in others | Directly in some, implied in others | Directly in all |

Table 1.—*Continued*

| Incident | Family | | |
|---|---|---|---|
| | English | Scottish | American |
| 10. A tells B that he could have married a king's daughter | Yes, except the fragment G | Yes, except version D (lines missing) | All but one |
| 11. B asks A about means of support | Yes, except the fragment | Yes, except version D | All but one |
| 12. A tells B he has ships, sailors, and gold | Yes, and B often wears gold slippers | Yes, except version D. Gold slippers mentioned in one | Yes; B dresses in rich apparel, usually gold |
| 13. B kisses children goodbye | Only in one | Yes, except D; husband, too, in one | Yes |
| 14. A and D go to sea | Yes | Yes | Yes |
| 15. B sees A's cloven feet | No in older; yes in more recent | Yes in older; no in more recent | No |
| 16. B regrets leaving | Yes, except broadside. B misses children and, in one, her husband | Yes; in one, she wants to die | Yes; in one, B wishes she had never been born (intrusive commonplace) |
| 17. A tells B about mountains of heaven and hell | Only one (version F) | Only one (version F) | Only one (version A) |

—*Continued*

Table 1. Families of "The Demon Lover" Ballad—*Continued*

| Incident | Family | | |
|---|---|---|---|
| | English | Scottish | American |
| 18. A tells B that he's going to punish her for breaking vows | No | Only one (version C) | No |
| 19. A sinks ship | No in earlier; in one, ship destroyed by fire; in another, ship disappears | Yes; in one, 2,500 ships perish | No; ship springs a leak |
| 20. B drowns | No in most; A and B in one | Yes; A throws her overboard in one | Yes |
| 21. C cries and hangs himself | Yes in broadside; swoons and cries in another; no in others | Cries in one; no in others | No |
| 22. Children left orphans | Only in broadside | No | No |
| 23. Lament or curses on mariners | Yes, C in earlier versions; no one in later | In one version, C curses sea, ship, mariners; no in others | In most, B curses mariners; in one, before she dies, but in most after she dies. |

*A, demon-lover; B, woman; C, carpenter.

side or, more likely, from other versions circulating at about the same time. As we have seen, some versions seem distinctly Scottish and others English. Although "The Demon Lover" has been referred to as a Scottish border ballad it is probably more accurate to say that the ballad traveled freely back and forth across the border and acquired characteristics common to ballads of both countries. Ballad collectors in the nineteenth century located idiosyncratic versions. All versions, however, have certain features of the plot formula in common; and yet strictly speaking, each differs from all other versions in some way. The earliest texts are dated many years apart, while more recent ones are dated within a few years of one another. The Child versions dated close together (C, D, E, and G) often differ significantly and yet contain characteristics of earlier texts, suggesting that families of ballads indeed circulated among the people of Great Britain during the nineteenth century.

Davis collected his versions in Virginia from 1914 to 1924. As compared with Scottish and English variants, the American versions are degenerate, as the plot formula is sketchy, all motivating elements have been deleted, and commonplaces from other ballads often intrude. The supernatural features found in British versions are missing in the American ones, but a new supernatural element is added. In many American texts, after the woman is drowned at the end of the ballad, she curses the sailor from her watery grave: "Oh, cursed be a sailor's life / And an o'er-persuading man / That stole me from my house carpenter / And took away my life" (Appendix B, version A). The cursing stanza resembles those in the broadside and in Peter Buchan's, except that, instead of the carpenter, the woman curses.

As Table 1 demonstrates, incidents one through eight are restricted to the broadside and, for the most part, incidents twenty-one through twenty-three are as well. In all of the later versions, a former lover explicitly or implicitly persuades her to go away with him; sometimes he is clearly a demon-lover and other times, especially in degenerate American variants, the lover is presumably real. Almost all versions of "The

Demon Lover" open with the conversation between the former lovers and end with the woman's death. Many versions retain key stanzas, especially those stanzas that relate the following: the returning lover tells the woman that he could have married a king's daughter, the woman asks the sailor about a means of support, he relates to her his supposed wealth, they go to sea, the woman expresses regret for having left home, the ship sinks (by supernatural or "natural" means). Because these stanzas are most likely to be retained, they comprise the basic plot formula and provide what Tristram P. Coffin calls "the emotional core."

Even though references to spirits and demons have diminished over time, it is important to remember the underlying supernatural context of the ballad. For instance, in some ways, it can be said that the history of "The Demon Lover" culminates with incident fifteen, the revelation of the cloven feet. The cloven-footed demon-lover first appeared in Scott's *Minstrelsy* and apparently was incorporated into oral tradition, or had been already, as evidenced by numerous later publications. In American versions, this element is dropped.

The history of any ballad follows a natural course: inception of the ballad in folk tradition; simplification of plot, dialogue, motivation; focusing of the "emotional core"; degeneration. Thus, the introduction and adoption of the demon-lover figure represents a consensus among both the folk and the collectors that the emotional core of this ballad is related to evil, fear, and violence. The natural course of any ballad dictates that certain features will be eliminated, others altered, while others will be added. At times, and this is true of "The Demon Lover," changes result in nonsense. American versions of the ballad, for example, involve lovers who are not appreciably demonic; without that quality the plot no longer has dramatic tension and the abduction of the woman no longer seems motivated by revenge. Without the temptation offered by a demon-lover, there is no way to explain why the woman abandons her family; and without the demon-destroyer, the woman's death is merely the result of an accident at sea.

The next chapter focuses first on the British Gothic tradition

and on vampire stories because of their dangerous and demonic associations. Then four works of fiction—*Wuthering
Heights, Tess of the d'Urbervilles*, "The Princess," and "The Demon Lover"—are explicated in light of their similarity to the
ballad.

# FOUR

# The Motif in
# British Fiction

But first, on earth as Vampire sent,
Thy corse shall from its tomb be rent:
Then ghostly haunt thy native place,
And such the blood of all thy race;
There from thy daughter, sister, wife,
At midnight drain the stream of life;
Yet loathe the banquet which perforce
Must feed thy livid living corse:
Thy victims ere they yet expire
Shall know the demon for their sire.

LORD BYRON
*The Giaour; A Fragment of a Turkish Tale*

The demon-lover figure represented in "The Demon Lover" ballad has evolved from ancient superstitions or, as some believe, from actual psychic experiences recorded in the collective unconscious of humankind. Tales of incubi, vampires, ghosts, and demons can be traced historically to the earliest stories ever recorded. Establishing whether there is any truth to these beliefs is beyond the scope of this investigation. Central to this study, however, is the recognition that imaginative portrayals of demon-lovers and victims have always been with us.

During the early centuries of the Roman Catholic Church, the subject of incubi and succubi was much debated. Many priests and nuns fell victim to nightly assaults from seductive creatures from the otherworld, although, as Nicolas Kiessling points out in his excellent study of incubi, the belief in supernatural nocturnal assaults was not widely held by Church leaders throughout Europe until about 1100 A.D. (*The Incubus in English Literature*, p. 21). Nevertheless, many priests were called upon to exorcise demons from those afflicted with persistent incubi or demon-lovers. Regarding the growing belief in demon molesters and the intervention of priests, Kiessling states:[18] "[M]any clerics heard vivid accounts of the incubus, and the stories of their foul deeds were legion. Even influential churchmen sometimes had firsthand experience with victims. Hincmar, Archbishop of Reims (845-880), writes of demons who deceive women in the form of lovers and gives an example of a nun who was freed from a demon lover by a priest who was a friend of his" (*Incubus* p. 22). Among superstitious people, stories of supernatural sexual assault circulated. Pregnant nuns, unwed mothers, and deformed children were blamed on night visitations by incubi. From the second through the eleventh centuries, beliefs about demon-lover figures abounded; mythological interpretations of Genesis 6:1-6 were introduced, and generally rejected, but never forgotten by the people (*Incubus*, p. 22). Folktales, ballads, and ultimately formal works of literature expressed a concern with demon-lover assaults.

Among the formal works of literature in the eighteenth century, Gothic novels best express the demon-lover motif that coincides with folk belief. Gothic literature may be thought of as dark romanticism; Elizabeth MacAndrew calls it the "literature of nightmare" (*The Gothic Tradition in Fiction*, p. 3), while Eino Railo calls it "horror-romanticism" (*The Haunted Castle*, p. 7). Gothicism has been an immensely popular form of literature since Horace Walpole, Anne Radcliffe, and Matthew G. Lewis established conventions for Gothicism in the eighteenth century. The Gothic novel, in fact, was the most popular kind of fiction in England from 1790 to 1820 (Coral Ann Howells, *Love, Mystery, and Misery*, p. 1), and its popularity remains strong to the present day.[19] The standard Gothic plot, complete with villain and victim, incorporates the underlying "emotional core" found in "The Demon Lover" ballad; Gothic romances, however, are generously embellished with props, settings, and special effects all designed to create an aura of anticipation and horror in readers. In a sense, the ballad is a distilled version of a Gothic romance about obsessive love and hate, for the woman in the ballad is just as controlled, just as victimized as the terrified women in *The Castle of Otranto, The Mysteries of Udolpho,* or Victoria Holt's *The Demon Lover.*

It has been said by Horace Walpole as well as by subsequent scholars that the most distinctive feature of Gothic literature is the emotional content. In general, Gothic literature penetrates our psyches in such a way that we respond on conscious and unconscious levels. Howells acknowledges the emotional impact on readers when she states, "As readers we are consistently placed in the position of literary voyeurs, always gazing at emotional excess without understanding the why of it: what we are given are the gestures of feeling rather than any insight into the complexity of the feelings themselves. The springs of these emotions elude us, so that we can only look on with appalled fascination as floods of feeling rush through the characters distorting their physical features with alarming rapidity" (pp. 15-16).

Gothic novelists deliberately promote emotional responses in readers by creating through their landscapes and props objective correlatives for the human passions: dark, damp castles; ruined abbeys; locked cellars and dungeons; secret passageways; creaking doors; rattling keys. Inner psychological states are evoked, and readers become "hooked" on the intensity generated by the stories told. Readers are fascinated by the resemblance of what happens in a Gothic novel to what happens in their own most private thoughts. Howells suggests this connection when she remarks, "If we look carefully under what at first glance appears an undifferentiated mass of sensationalism we shall see a number of remarkable attempts to explore the private hinterland of the human personality. These explorations are expressed through intense and exaggerated imagery in which contemporary readers found excitement, suspense and beneath it all an interplay of the passions they covertly recognized in themselves as sharing" (p. 27).

Specifically, the emotions typically experienced by readers of Gothic fiction are terror, pain, and sexual excitement. As Linda Bayer-Berenbaum suggests, "In terror a person feels powerfully present, starkly alive" (*The Gothic Imagination*, p. 31). She further suggests that fear is the essential Gothic emotion and that "the victim in the story, as well as the reader, is overawed by the conqueror" (p. 44). Fear or terror results, then, from a close identification with the victimization depicted in the story. Because Gothic tales are presented through sensual imagery, identification is enhanced; readers *experience* the darkness, the sweep of a vampire bat, the rattling of chains, the slammed door, and the rape.

Many Gothic novels deal with pain, torture, sadism and masochism; in the dark, sinister gothic setting presented, only one's *nightmares* come true, only the oppressive power of the night, the incubi of one's imagination. "Agony, or the attempt to imagine it," Bayer-Berenbaum states, "is a very effective technique for intensifying perception; in that the suffering person desperately desires relief, pain is an instant cure for apathy and insensitivity, passivity and moderation, the enemies of the Gothic spirit" (p. 30).

In Gothic works, aberrant sexuality is often presented hand in hand with terror and pain. Sexual desire on the part of the would-be lover is obsessive and destructive, while the victim is often presented as virginal—a combination that sets up a demon-lover arrangement whereby the lover accosts the victim, renders her will subservient to his, then destroys her purity, her sanity, or her life. This behavioral pattern is remarkably similar to the one found in "The Demon Lover" ballad. Aberrant sexuality in Gothic literature is often associated with supernatural beings—demons, vampires, witches, or men with an uncanny power to control. This connection between sexuality and the supernatural in Gothic fiction seems clearly related to the sexual orgies attributed to witches and the Devil. In any case, sexual tension is a physiological and emotional response experienced by many readers of Gothic novels. Writers of erotic fiction during the eighteenth and nineteenth centuries, writers whose work is often couched in Gothic imagery, are more straightforward in their attempts to elicit sexual response from their readers than writers of Gothic fiction, who promote sexual excitement through symbols of dangerous and forbidden acts denied by the conscious mind. Perhaps some readers require an exaggerated stimulus in order to respond at all; perhaps sexual response to aberrant sexual behavior is preferable to no response at all. As Bayer-Berenbaum remarks, "Sexual excess functions physically as madness does psychologically; one drive, one intention, becomes overpowering, all-consuming" (pp. 39-40). Gothic fiction promotes exaggerated emotional responses which lead to intensified feelings.

Supernatural elements in Gothic novels produce a nameless dread in readers; the terror of the unknown comes alive to destroy peace and harmony. Gothic conventions provide opportunities for juxtaposing images of heaven and hell, the sacred and the perverse. Cathedrals, spires, and supernatural light, suggestive of grace, all connote the possibility of spiritual transcendence. The Gothic vision, however, affirms the power of darkness; man's sinfulness, his perversity of spirit, pervades the landscape and inscape of the tales told. Bayer-Berenbaum suggests a connection between the popularity of Gothic novels and declining religious sensibility when she states, "The rise of the Gothic Novel may itself be related to religious depravity in that Gothic practices provide a cathartic outlet for the sense of guilt that accompanies the decline of a strong religion, the horrors in the novel serving as a release for repressed fears" (p. 37).

Critics of Gothic literature have commented on the cathartic possibilities inherent in a genre that taps into the unconscious realms of the mind. Howells suggests that Gothic novelists create "anthropomorphized evil in the form of Satan, devils, ghosts, lamia, incubi, succubi, vampires, and ghouls" in their attempts to symbolize what she calls "a Christian iconography of fallen man" (p. 6), i.e., an "eternal victim—victim of both himself and of something outside himself" (p. 7). The religious undercurrent in Gothic fiction, then, opposes the dominant urge to destroy and creates the tension between good and evil.

In Gothic fiction, there is an unmistakable attraction to ruin, decay, and death. Bayer-Berenbaum suggests that to concentrate on death and destruction is to express a general abhorrence of restriction (p. 28), and, in the same way, focusing on sexual perversion means transcending moral restrictions. In the Gothic worlds depicted by Walpole, Radcliffe, Lewis, and others, unpredictability, insecurity, instability, fear, and powerlessness are counteracted by power. Usually there is one character who is all-powerful and seems to work in harmony with the demonic force that appears to control events. Thus, Gothic literature expresses the tensions between powerlessness and power, between aggression and victimization. Regarding the cathartic power of Gothic fiction to prepare us for our own deaths, Bayer-Berenbaum remarks, "Death and sickness lead us to acknowledge the extent of the forces that control us, and in the face of death we recognize the omnipotence of time and try to confront our own annihilation. The concept of self-extinction stretches consciousness; we probe the limits of our minds with fear, with caution, and yet with a certain thrill" (p. 26).

Vampire stories have fascinated and terrified readers for generations. This type of Gothic tale is perfectly suited for transcending moral limitations related to sexuality, religion, and death. Bayer-Berenbaum clarifies the unique state of deathlessness held by vampires: "Ghosts and vampires are rejections of time in that they live on indefinitely, and wraiths (apparitions of living people) are in the same sense rejections of temporal and spatial limitation. . . The recurrent Gothic theme of the living dead or the dead alive strains the distinction between (and thus the limitations of) life and death in a manner parallel to the way the physical and spiritual realms overlap" (p. 33). Vampires have a marginal status, for they are neither dead nor alive; thus, they represent a victory over death. But because, theoretically, vampires are immortal, they bring infinite destruction into the world, and that of course is the horror of vampirism: eternal victimization. Vampires represent a perversion of the Christian belief in the afterlife, but rather than ascending to heaven after death, vampires return to victimize the living by drawing the life force out of them, by sucking their blood, and by producing more vampires, i.e., by reproducing themselves.

Vampires supposedly join "the living dead" as a result of some great crime committed while alive, and they are thought to victimize those they loved the most while on earth. Some occultists and researchers actually believe that vampires roam the earth today and have always done so and that stories of actual vampirism have been suppressed over the years. Montague Summers, who studied the question of vampirism in great depth, states in *The Vampire: His Kith and Kin* that he believes in vampires and that evidence has indeed been predictably suppressed in today's rational world. Moreover, he provides support for the possibility of the phenomenon in the following historical note: "Towards the end of the seventeenth century, and even more particularly during the first half of the eighteenth century . . . in Hungary, Moravia, and Galicia, there seemed to be a veritable epidemic of vampirism the report of which was bruited far and wide engaging the attention of curia and university ecclesiatic and philosopher, scholar and man of letters" (*Vampire*, p. xxii). Historically, concern with vampirism in Europe at the end of the seventeenth century and at the beginning of the eighteenth coincides perfectly with the oral dissemination' of "The Demon Lover" in Scotland and England; and, as demonstrated in chapter 2, folktales, beliefs, and superstitions about demon-destroyers were also pervasive at this time. As a motif, the demon-lover has appeared in many forms but its popularity is uncontestable.

By the nineteenth century, works of literature were being written describing the activities of vampires in gruesome detail. In 1819, *The New Monthly Magazine* published John William Polidori's *The Vampyre: a Tale by Lord Byron*, which created a sensation in England; although it was widely known that Byron had not written the work, it has been included in many collections of Byron's work until recent years. *The Vampire* was subsequently translated into French and German and gained great popularity in Europe (Summers, *Vampire*, pp. 280 and 290). During the early nineteenth century, vampire stories were turned into plays that were extremely popular in London and Paris. In 1847, James Malcolm Rymer's *Varney the Vampire, or, The Feast of Blood*, the first full-length literary work about vampires, was published and proved to be so popular that it was reissued in 1853 in penny parts (Summers, *Vampire*, p. 333).[20]

By far the most widely read of all vampire stories is Bram Stoker's *Dracula*, first published in 1897. C.F. Bentley was among the first to acknowledge the sexual symbolism in *Dracula*, pointing out (in "The Monster in the Bedroom: Sexual Symbolism in Bram Stoker's *Dracula*") that Victorian readers were undaunted by the sadistic suffering of the innocent perpetrated by Dracula and apparently oblivious to the covert sexual perversity in the novel. Bentley makes an excellent case for the repressed sexual content of Stoker's work, citing as one example the tableau in Mina Harker's bedroom when Dracula forces her to drink his blood:

> By her side stood a tall, thin man, clad in black. His face was turned from us, but the instant we saw we all recognized the Count—in every way, even to the scar on his forehead. With his left hand he held both Mrs. Harker's hands, keeping them away with her arms at full tension; his right hand gripped her by the back of the neck, forcing her face down on his bosom. Her white nightdress was smeared with blood, and a thin stream trickled down the man's bare breast which was shown by his torn-open dress. The attitude of the two had a terrible resemblance to a child forcing a kitten's nose into a saucer of milk to compel it to drink. [ch. XXI; p. 289]

Bentley suggests that blood is a substitute for semen in *Dracula*, pointing out (in "The Monster in the Bedroom: Sexual Symbolism in Bram Stoker's *Dracula*") that Victorian readers were undaunted by the sadistic suffering of the innocent per-the above scene, Bentley suggests that Stoker "is describing a symbolic act of enforced fellatio, where blood is again a substitute for semen, and where a chaste female suffers a violation that is essentially sexual" (p. 30). The typical act of a vampire, sucking blood from a beautiful young woman's neck, or in this case, forcing the woman to suck his blood, is an invasion, a sublimated sexual attack; by forcing the woman to submit to his will, Dracula symbolically rapes her. The sexual terror and excitement presented in *Dracula* produces a powerful Gothic drama: the sexual aggression, the sense of moral danger, and the violated innocence repeat the same archetypal pattern etched in the human collective unconscious, to which the prevalence of the motif testifies. We are both horrified by and fascinated with vampires, and with Dracula in particular as he appears to be a civilized villain, a rake, in the midst of chaos and utter destruction. In *Dracula*, the movement from primitive Transylvania to late nineteenth-century London results in a modern-day confrontation with the supernatural. Dracula only *seems* civilized, however, as his preternatural desire to possess women, to penetrate them with his teeth, condemns his victims to eternal participation in barbaric necrophilic rites from which they cannot escape. Vampire stories, then, are far more terrifying than other Gothic tales because once claimed by their destroyer-lovers, victims are held forever in a powerful trance that obviates freedom. In *Dracula*, the life-and-death struggle for possession of Lucy Westenra's soul that takes place between Dracula and Dr. Van Helsing is symbolized by alternate blood sucking and blood transfusions. In sexual terms, Lucy's life-threatening struggle involves the temptation of bestial seduction and the purity of reinstated "virginity" *vis à vis* penetration by Dracula's fangs. To be consumed by Dracula, to be seduced successfully, means that she must die.

Several critics have speculated that *Dracula* expresses a repression of sexuality by Victorians. Judith Weissman proposes that Stoker creates prototypical nymphomaniacs who break free of all constraints and taboos, and that in the end a small coterie of gallant men reestablish the natural order by releasing Dracula's erotic hold upon the women, thereby restoring their purity, their virginity. Weissman refers to *Dracula* as "a great horror story and a very extreme version of the

myth that there are two types of woman, devils and angels"
("Women and Vampires," p. 397). As Weissman points out,
Van Helsing is clearly the champion of virtue in the novel,
the hero who delivers most of the major dialogue regarding
the purity and passivity of women. According to this view of
the novel, Stoker presents the danger of sexual excess (by
women), demonstrates the power of reason to conquer the
supernatural, and provides a means for virginity and love to
emerge victorious. All of this is accomplished despite the ancient tradition of vampires. The cat-and-mouse game that Dracula and Van Helsing play in London and Transylvania
signifies perhaps the sexual ambivalence undoubtedly within
Stoker and within many of his contemporary readers as well.

Basing his interpretation on the social isolation of Dracula,
Burton Hatlen offers a Marxist reading of the novel by suggesting that "Count Dracula represents . . . the repressed
and the oppressed: the psychically repressed and the socially
oppressed" ("The Return of the Repressed/Oppressed," p.
82). Quoting Frederick Jameson's article "Magical Narratives:
Romance as Genre," Hatlen establishes Count Dracula as a
villain created by social determinism:

"It is becoming increasingly clear that the concept of evil
is at one with the category of Otherness itself: evil char-
acterizes whatever is radically different from me, whatever by virtue of precisely that difference seems to
constitute a very real and urgent threat to my existence.
So from earliest times, the stranger from another tribe,
the 'barbarian' who speaks an incomprehensible language and follows 'outlandish' customs, or, in our own
day, the avenger of cumulated resentments from some
oppressed class, or else that alien being—Jew or Communist—behind whose apparently human features an
intelligence of a malignant and preternatural superiority
is thought to lurk—these are some of the figures in
which the fundamental identity of the representative of
Evil and the Other are [sic] visible. The point, however,
is not that in such figures the Other is feared because

he is evil; rather he is evil *because* he is Other, alien, different, strange, unclean, and unfamiliar." [p. 82; Hatlen's *sic*]

This view of Count Dracula implies that he is a villain *because* he is an outsider and responds to alienation with destructive, vicious behavior. As the representative of sexual excess, Dracula has a mesmerizing effect upon women, freeing them from moral constraints which inhibit their sexual passion. Hatlen explains the morbid attraction to Dracula experienced in the novel by Lucy and Mina: "Denied by Victorian society an opportunity to express their sexuality openly, Lucy and Mina find in Count Dracula an 'objective correlative' of their lost sexuality; and blindly, unconsciously they give themselves to their demon lover" (p. 85). The only thing required of these women, Hatlen goes on to suggest, is their passive submission to Dracula's power. As he penetrates their vulnerable necks with his phallic teeth, they are held captive and powerless until he has completely exhausted their wills; once they are under his command, they too become sexual deviants who seek to seduce and conquer others. "Insofar as Count Dracula incarnates our lost sexuality," Hatlen maintains, "he becomes the shape not only of our most terrible fears but also of our deepest desires. He is the other that we cannot escape, because he is part of us. He is the other that we loathe *and* love (p. 87). In Victorian society, Hatlen implies, the very existence of sexual repression results in a tension between constraint and self-abandonment, between virginity and nymphomania, all of which is symbolized very well by vampirism.

As Hatlen reminds us, Dracula "is apparently about four hundred years old, and thus he is a *revenant* from a pre-enlightenment world" (p. 88). The Count represents primordial instincts which can be counteracted only by symbols such as crucifixes and Communion wafers; Dracula himself can be destroyed only by an equally symbolic stake pounded into his heart. Encounters with Dracula have an unmistakable sexual quality to them and always lead to death. This connection between sexuality and death is typical of all demon-lover tales. The sexual obsession and the abdication of the victim's will expressed in *Dracula* create a plot that is similar to the one found in "The Demon Lover" complex. Both Count Dracula and the demon-lover of the ballad stalk their victims; Dracula attacks his victims by biting their necks, thereby immobilizing them, while in the ballad the conniving demon-lover tricks the woman into accompanying him to her death. Images of the mountains of heaven and hell found in the ballad may be compared to the sexual ecstasy and the eternal restlessness presented in *Dracula*. Count Dracula's castle, furthermore, stands at the top of a dark, mysterious mountain shrouded in fog, and what happens there seems hellish indeed, according to Jonathon Harker's eyewitness account. The attraction and repulsion experienced by victims for their demon-lovers, a characteristic typical of virtually all literary works based on the demon-lover motif, can be explained by the association of sexuality with death, as exemplified so well by Stoker's *Dracula*. Sexual ecstasy at times involves a dissolving of ego boundaries or a temporary annihilation of one's identity which may seem like death. As a representative of primordial instincts or of the human libido, Count Dracula threatens rationality and moral propriety; thus, as women's sexual instincts increase, their survival instincts decrease, resulting in vampirization of unwilling yet yielding victims. In the ballad as well, the victim seems unwilling yet acquiescent as she falls under the mesmerizing influence of her demon-destroyer, recklessly dashing off to her demise. Just as the woman in the ballad feels compelled by the power of her demon-lover, Lucy Westenra, clearly attracted to Dracula, waits for his return, although horrified at the thought of succumbing to his power.

As we have seen in chapter 2, demon-lover figures are related to Satan, who characteristically deceives and destroys his victims. Count Dracula clearly resembles Satan in several important ways: his dark sinister appearance—the dark complexion and the black clothes and cape; his rank odor; the fact that he comes in the night to his victims' windows (and must be let in by the women in the same way that witches characteristically give Satan permission to enter). In many ways Dracula is a prototype of the Antichrist: his obsession with blood and flesh seems a perversion of the Eucharist, his aversion to the crucifix implies a rejection of Christ, and his affinity with the night suggests his identity as the Prince of Darkness. *Dracula*, a Gothic melodrama, essentially reveals the same aggressor/victim interaction present in works of literature throughout the centuries. In fiction, the earliest and certainly the most influential demon-lover figure is Lovelace. In *Clarissa*, Samuel Richardson creates a sophisticated rake who, like Count Dracula, becomes pathologically fixated on an innocent, virginal woman, subsequently besieges her, and eventually rapes her.

In her famous essay on Richardson's novel, Dorothy Van Ghent downplays the importance of the rape, stating, "The central event of the novel, over which the interminable series of letters hovers so cherishingly, is, considered in the abstract, a singularly thin and unrewarding piece of action—the deflowering of a young lady—and one which scarcely seems to deserve the universal uproar which it provokes in the book. There is very little subplot. The rape is in the offing, it is at hand, it is here, it is over, Clarissa sickens and dies, and that is all" (p. 47). Such an unsympathetic view of Clarissa's suffering indicates that Van Ghent places the emphasis of the novel elsewhere. In her essay, she establishes the mythical dimensions of Lovelace and Clarissa, suggesting that the universal appeal of Richardson's novel depends upon our recognizing the human struggle between good and evil. Van Ghent sees Lovelace and Clarissa as symbols which serve a mythical purpose, symbols which evolve from a series of images of these characters. Lovelace represents "the man," or the sexual threat, and "as the image grows by reiteration and variation into a symbol," Van Ghent suggests, "attractive elements are fused with the repellent elements, so that the abominable toadlike reptilian 'man' becomes demonically fascinating: a creature obsessed with the desire to violate virginal, high-minded, helpless womanhood, and so single-tracked in his passion to destroy this divinity that he, too, assumes divine stature: he is the evil divinity, the devil himself" (p. 51).

She describes Clarissa in equally colorful language as she clarifies the fundamental basis for this character's appeal: "Her mythical features still appear to us—for it would be a mistake to think that the Clarissa-myth does not still have deep social and psychological roots—in her two chief aspects: they appear on the covers of *Vogue* magazine, in the woman who is a wraith of clothes, debile and expensive, irrelevant to sense-life or affectional life, to be seen only; and they appear on the covers of *True Confessions* and *True Detective Stories*, in the many-breasted woman with torn dishabille and rolling eyeballs, a dagger pointing at her . . . Clarissa is a powerful symbol because she is both" (pp. 50-51). Although Van Ghent fails to make the observation, Richardson alludes to this two-fold quality of Clarissa's character with the name *Harlowe*, which seems a subtle confluence of associations, harlot and halo. Clarissa's name lends further support to the view that as a victim, she is both willing and unwilling, both repelled by and fascinated with her demon-lover.

In a more recent study, Terry Eagleton explains Lovelace's extreme preoccupation with Clarissa in Freudian terms. Lovelace, he asserts, feels a deep ambivalence toward Clarissa, the "phallic woman," who is to him a substitute for his castrated mother. Because of his Oedipal anxiety, Lovelace must possess Clarissa in order to restore his own power, for according to this critic, "Daunted by her 'phallic' wholeness, shaken by this nameless threat to his own gender, Lovelace must possess Clarissa so that he may reunite himself with the lost phallus, and unmask her as reassuringly 'castrated.' Indeed by ritually exposing all women in turn, he may compulsively reassure himself that they are all indeed 'castrated.' All of them will be revealed as worthless, as easy prey to desire, in contrast with the one unattainable woman—the mother—who is beyond desire altogether" (*The Rape of Clarissa*, p. 58). Eagleton goes on to identify as personal blind spots Clarissa's lack of self-awareness as well as her attraction for Lovelace and her lover's sexual idolization of her, stating that "Clarissa and Lovelace are equally cocooned in false consciousness, mutually thwarting and travestying" (p. 68). But these blind spots that Eagleton identifies are precisely what the archetypal demon-lover/victim relationship is composed of: heightened sexual energy, diminished rationality, and lack of self-discipline.

As Richardson demonstrated well over two hundred years ago, the drama inherent in a demon-lover/victim interaction is perfectly suited to the narrative format of fiction. During the early nineteenth century, when the novel as a genre was taking shape, "The Demon Lover" circulated widely, providing, it seems, the underlying plot structure for the works of many authors from that point forward. Literary artists, along with the general population, gradually shifted from a Romantic, idealized vision of the universe to a more realistic one that encompassed a growing awareness of corruption and evil; as a motif, the demon-lover conflict combines a Romantic view of love with terror, for according to the plot formula represented by the ballad, the conflict is consistently resolved through violence.

Stoker's *Dracula* captures the collective struggle between the Victorian ideal of purity and the human urge to express passion. As in *Clarissa* and "The Demon Lover," *Dracula* relies on the dramatic tension between victim and victimizer. In demon-lover tales, innocence and the Romantic ideal as conveyed by the victims are overpowered by the violence perpetrated by their demon-lovers. It is possible, then, that the demon-lover motif served a social function in England during a time of major change in world view.

Two other major nineteenth-century British novels explore destructive love relationships that fit the plot formula found in the ballad: Emily Brontë's *Wuthering Heights* and Thomas Hardy's *Tess of the d'Urbervilles*. These two works share an affinity with *Clarissa*, as Lovelace is the literary prototype after which Heathcliff and Alec d'Urberville are patterned. Pointing out the similarity between Heathcliff and his predecessor

Lovelace, Van Ghent remarks, "The daemonic character of Heathcliff, associated as it is with the wildness of heath and moors, has a recognizable kinship with that of Lovelace, daemonic also, though associated with town life and sophisticated manners. Both are, essentially, an anthropomorphized primitive energy, concentrated in activity, terrible in effect" (p. 154). Tess Durbeyfield shares certain qualities with Clarissa Harlowe and, to a lesser degree, Catherine Earnshaw-Linton, but both nineteenth-century novels essentially duplicate the obsessive-compulsive love-hate interaction found in its purest form in the ballad.

Certainly most British novelists during the nineteenth century had been exposed to ballads. Emily Brontë mentions "Chevy Chase" by name in *Wuthering Heights*, and her proximity to the Scottish border makes it extremely likely that she was familiar with other border ballads such as "The Demon Lover." G.D. Klingopulos points out the balladlike quality of *Wuthering Heights* when he remarks, "It has anonymity. It is not complete. Perhaps some ballads represent it in English, but it seldom appears in the main stream, and few writers are in touch with it" (quoted by Van Ghent, p. 153). Perhaps the fact that the novel resembles a ballad in its folkloric presentation explains the difficulty literary critics have consistently had in trying to define or categorize the work. G. Malcolm Laws has compiled the following list of characteristics of folk ballads, a list helpful for establishing the similarity of *Wuthering Heights* to balladry:

1) Impersonality of expression (the author remains far in the background);
2) Simple, unaffected folk language (poetic diction is not usually at home in the ballads);
3) Familiar and evocative imagery (the ballad cliché is highly connotative);
4) Succinctness (the ballad story leaves much unsaid);
5) Direct and violent actions and reactions (ballad characters are uninhibited);
6) Dramatization rather than summary of events (bal-

lads are miniature plays which use much dialogue).
[Laws, *British,* P. 59]

The balladlike quality of the novel suggests the provocative
idea that the narrator, Lockwood, serves as a ballad singer
who begins his song in a typical fashion: "I once heard a tale
about. . . ." Nelly Dean is the source of Lockwood's tale and
a participant in the story, an arrangement common to ballad
narratives. A close look at the novel reveals a structural kinship with "The Demon Lover," for the same type of irrational,
obsessive love and hate expressed in the ballad is found in
Brontë's novel.

Heathcliff, as much an outsider as Dracula, seems to promote himself throughout the novel as demonic, for his behavior consistently causes others to view him so. Regarding
his demonic nature, Van Ghent states, "Heathcliff's is an
archetypal figure, untraceably ancient in mythological
thought—an imaged recognition of that part of nature which
is 'other' than the human soul (the world of the elements and
the animals) and of that part of the soul itself which is 'other'
than the conscious part" (p. 163). In "Heathcliff as Vampire,"
James Twitchell argues that over the years critics have become
increasingly sympathetic toward Heathcliff, citing James Hafley's contention in "The Villain of *Wuthering Heights*" that
Nelly Dean is the *real* villain of the novel. Twitchell argues
that Heathcliff should again be seen as the devil he is and
that Brontë meant for him to have the qualities of a vampire,
a mythological figure with which nineteenth-century readers
could easily identify: "I do not mean to imply that Heathcliff
*is* a vampire, but only that his relationships with other people
can be explained metaphorically and that the metaphor Emily
Brontë developed was one of parasite and host, oppressor
and victim, vampire and vampirized" (p. 356). Close analysis
of the novel, of the references to Heathcliff as demonic, supports Twitchell's position.

At the beginning of the novel, by the time Mr. Lockwood
asks Nelly to tell him about Heathcliff, he has already formed
his own opinion of the man. In a diary he keeps, Lockwood

describes Heathcliff as "a dark-skinned gypsy . . . rather morose" (Brontë, p. 15), and records that his landlord "revealed a genuine bad nature" and speaks "with an almost diabolical sneer on his face" (p. 20). Nelly begins the history of Heathcliff's life at Wuthering Heights by relating the effect Heathcliff had on people as a child. When old Mr. Earnshaw presents Heathcliff (an orphan he has "found" in Liverpool) to his family, he calls the boy "a gift from God, though it's dark almost as if it came from the devil" (p. 38). Hindley Earnshaw hates Heathcliff from the start and calls him an "Imp of Satan" (p. 41). Nelly also tells Lockwood about the incident at Thrushcross Grange when Heathcliff and Catherine are caught spying on the Linton children; the children's father (according to what Heathcliff told Nelly at the time) asks, "would it not be a kindness to the country to hang him [Heathcliff] at once, before he shows his nature in acts, as well as features?" (p. 49). Nelly explains that Heathcliff "bred bad feelings" (p. 40) at Wuthering Heights from the moment he arrived, clearly suggesting that Heathcliff is a destructive, demonic force introduced into an otherwise peaceful home. At one point Nelly relates a conversation she once had with young Heathcliff, during which she said to him: "Do you mark those lines between your eyes; and those thick brows, that instead of rising arched, sink in the middle; and that couple of black fiends, so deeply buried, who never open their windows boldly, but lurk glinting under them, like devil's spies?" (p. 54). Early in the novel, then, Brontë establishes Heathcliff as a demonic figure, and although she is careful to provide precipitating causes of Heathcliff's pernicious behavior, he is nevertheless presented as a dark, destructive force. His behavior, as reported by every other character in the work, indicts him.

In most versions of the ballad, a vow exchanged between the two former lovers is implicitly or explicitly mentioned. Heathcliff and Catherine Earnshaw exchanged vows, in a sense, as children, for as Nelly tells Lockwood, "They both promised fair to grow up as rude as savages" (p. 46). While Heathcliff becomes obsessively jealous of the time Catherine spends with other people, she becomes exceedingly cruel. To support this view, Nelly recreates for Lockwood a scene during which Catherine tells Nelly that although she loves Heathcliff she will marry Edgar Linton. Catherine begins by revealing a prophetic dream she had in which she was, significantly, flung out of heaven "into the middle of the *heath* on the top of Wuthering Heights; where I woke sobbing for joy" (p. 72; my emphasis).

After Heathcliff overhears Catherine's avowal to marry Edgar, he goes away for three years, Nelly reports—the same length of time that the lovers in many of the ballad texts are separated. When he returns, the changes in him are startling. Nelly remembers his dark face, dark hair, and mustache, and his dark clothes, but most of all, she remembers his deep-set eyes "full of black fire" (p. 84). Shortly after Heathcliff returns, Catherine complains to Nelly that the last seven years seem a blank and that her misery began when she was separated from Heathcliff following her convalescence at Thrushcross Grange, four years before Heathcliff left Wuthering Heights. After her return from the Grange, Nelly recalls, Catherine adopted "a double character without exactly intending to deceive anyone" (p. 62). From this point on (until she goes mad), Catherine is more "civilized," more manageable, and yet still compelled to love Heathcliff above all else. During an exchange between the lovers, Heathcliff says that Catherine has treated him "infernally" and that he seeks revenge, to which Catherine responds, "Well, I won't repeat my offer of a wife: it is as bad as offering Satan a lost soul. Your bliss lies, like his, in inflicting misery" (p. 97).

Shortly after this, Catherine becomes ill to the point of madness. In a crucial speech to Nelly, Catherine provides an important insight into her psychological makeup: "Nelly, I'll tell you what I thought. . . . that I was enclosed in the oak-panelled bed at home; . . . the whole last seven years of my life grew a blank! I did not recall that they had been at all. I was a child; my father was just buried, and my misery arose from the separation that Hindley had ordered between me and Heathcliff. . . . I wish I were a girl again, half savage,

and hardy, and free; and laughing at injuries, not maddening
under them! Why am I so changed?" (p. 107).

As she talks to Nelly she sees a candle in her bedroom
window at Wuthering Heights and wants to return, symbolically, by way of the graveyard; she then swears that when
she dies she will not rest until Heathcliff is dead and buried
as well (p. 108).

The above passage reminds us of Lockwood's nightmarish
experience early in the novel when he spends the night in
that same oak-panelled bed at Wuthering Heights:

"Let me in—let me in!"
"Who are you? . . . "
"Catherine Linton. . . . I'm come home. I'd lost my
way on the moor!"
As it spoke, I discerned, obscurely, a child's face looking through the window. . . .
" . . . that minx, Catherine Linton, or Earnshaw, or
however she was called—she must have been a changeling—wicked little soul! She told me she had been
walking the earth these twenty years." [pp. 30-32]

Interestingly, Lockwood sees Catherine as a lost child. This
suggests that Emily Brontë believed, as many people do, that
ghosts are manifestations of psychic disturbances. The "double character" that Catherine assumed upon returning from
Thrushcross Grange after her convalescence could have resulted from profound psychic vulnerability. Thus, at that
time, she might have formed an unnatural identification with
Heathcliff, frozen and locked in time.

The lovers' passionate parting scene which Nelly recreates
for Lockwood provides a clearer understanding of the obsessive love and hate that Catherine and Heathcliff feel for each
other. During the several minutes that the lovers embrace,
they accuse each other, and their embrace turns into physical
cruelty. "I wish I could hold you . . . till we were both dead!"
(p. 133), Catherine says. Clutching her arm savagely and leaving four distinct bruises on her, he asks, "Are you possessed

with a devil . . . ?'' (p. 133), and clings to Catherine intensely, "like a mad dog" (p. 134).

Early the next morning, Catherine dies. Several years after her death, Heathcliff tells Nelly that on the night Catherine was buried he dug up her grave to see her once more, and he arranged with the gravedigger to remove the adjoining sides of her casket and his own when he is finally buried beside her, thereby allowing a total merger of their bodies and spirits. Interestingly, the mingling of souls is represented in several popular ballads as well, by flowers and briars intertwined on graves, an association which makes *Wuthering Heights* seem closely aligned with several ballads with which Brontë's readers would have been familiar.[21]

For the next eighteen years, Heathcliff restlessly seeks Catherine's ghost; he seeks, in a sense, his own demonic likeness, his own lost soul which he believes Catherine took to the grave with her. Eventually, Nelly explains somewhat skeptically to Lockwood, Heathcliff begins to "see" his long-departed Catherine, and she begins to communicate "both pleasure and pain, in exquisite extremes" (p. 261). Heathcliff remains receptive to his vision and obedient to the inaudible directives which lead to his death, or so it seems to Nelly. The narrator recalls her thoughts on the night that Heathcliff slept in Catherine's oak-paneled bed—the night before he died: " 'Is he a ghoul, or a vampire?' I mused. I had read of such hideous, incarnate demons" (p. 260).

Earlier in the novel, Nelly tells Lockwood that five days after Catherine died, Isabella escaped from Wuthering Heights, where Heathcliff had tormented her since they were married. In her conversation with Nelly, Isabella provides us with an important insight into Heathcliff's spiritual desolation when she reports to Nelly the nature of his prayers following Catherine's burial: "He has just come home at dawn, and gone upstairs to his chamber; locking himself in. . . . There he has continued, praying like a Methodist; only the deity he implored is senseless dust and ashes; and God, when addressed, was curiously confounded with his own black father!'' (pp. 143-44). Heathcliff, the orphan—the abandoned, unreclaimed "dark gypsy"—seems determined to reject God as he believes he was rejected by his own father. Rebellion against God, Brontë suggests, leads to alienation, despair, and self-destruction. As a demon-lover figure, Heathcliff directly facilitates Catherine's spiritual downfall by seducing her into a world of psychic devastation. Typical of victims involved in a demon-lover conflict, Catherine is both attracted to and repelled by Heathcliff. Over time, however, Catherine becomes weaker as her will and her life collapse under the strain of his obsession with her.

At the end of the novel, Joseph concludes, looking into Heathcliff's dead face, "Th' divil's harried off his soul . . . !" (p. 264). By the time Heathcliff dies at the end of *Wuthering Heights*, Brontë has prepared us to accept the lovers' reunion on the moors. Thus, after death the two lovers, like medieval ghosts, are bound to the earth through their obsession with one another; they lack the freedom to let go of this world, to enter spiritual realms.

Brontë was evidently fascinated with obsession in relationships. In *Wuthering Heights*, she carefully presents several causal factors leading to the utter destruction of two human beings who failed to recognize the self-defeating patterns of interaction in which they were engaged. She establishes Heathcliff's mysterious origin, his orphan status in the Earnshaw family, the hateful behavior he endured as a child, his early possessiveness towards Catherine, their separation as children and later as young adults, Heathcliff's vindictive response and Catherine's desire to please him. In any novel, precipitating factors are often introduced, while in a short ballad, motivation is seldom provided; instead, events are reported objectively, as they are in newspaper accounts of crime. In her novel, Emily Brontë engenders a demon-lover tale more complex than the ballad, as hers provides glimpses into the psychological makeup of the two lovers—the genesis of hate and the propensity toward victimization.

Thomas Hardy's *Tess of the d'Urbervilles* also repeats the underlying plot structure found in the ballad. Hardy incorporates numerous lines from ballads in his novel, allowing those lines to anticipate or to emphasize new developments in the plot. When Tess returns home after the May-walking, she hears her mother singing one of her favorite ballads, "The Spotted Cow": "I saw her lie do'—own in yon'—der green gro'—ove; / Come, love!' and I'll tell' you where!' " (Hardy, p. 56). The image anticipates Tess's violation in the green grove the night that Alec takes advantage of her innocence and weariness. After the birth of her illegitimate child, Tess works in the fields of Marlott and nurses her baby; and on one occasion, the other field hands, we are told, "could not refrain from mischieviously throwing in a few verses of the ballad about the maid who went to the merry green wood and came back a changed state" (p. 142).

Tess is often identified with cows in the novel. She first arrives at Talbothays in the Valley of the Great Dairies precisely at half past four o'clock, milking time, and falls in with the herd of cows, slowly walking behind them toward the milking barn. She joins the others in milking the cows, although Dairyman Crick soon exclaims that the cows seem to be holding back, to which another dairyman suggests that because there is a newcomer (Tess) among them, the cows are not giving their milk. As a cure for the cows' condition, Crick recommends that someone sing ballads to them, for, we are told, "Songs were often resorted to in dairies hereabout as an enticement to the cows when they showed signs of withholding their usual yield" (p. 164). So to this end they sing "fourteen or fifteen verses of a cheerful ballad about a murderer who was afraid to go to bed in the dark because he saw certain brimstone flames around him," a ballad that forewarns of danger and murder. At this point in the story, Tess and Angel meet. This ballad serves to release milk from the cows and love from Tess, it seems, and much of the initial lovemaking that occurs between Angel and her is initiated while milking the cows. Later in the novel, Angel buys Tess her wedding ensemble, and when she stands before her mirror looking at herself, "her mother's ballad of the mystic robe" comes to mind: "That never would become that wife / That had once done amiss" (p. 272). We are told that Tess had not

thought of that ballad until that moment since she had been
at the dairy. The lines from the ballad encapsulate Tess's situation: because of her past sexual experience with Alec, though
against her will, she was to become Angel's wife in name
only. This ballad prophesies Tess's future.
Consistent with the prophecy of the mystic-robe ballad,
Angel leaves Tess and goes to Brazil. While he is there, Tess
prepares for his return by learning his favorite ballads, hoping
to please him. She works especially hard to perfect "The break
o' the day," a sentimental ballad that expresses her wistful-
ness:

> Arise, arise, arise!
> And pick your love a posy,
> All o' the sweetest flowers
> That in the garden grow.
> The turtle doves and sma' birds
> In every bough a-building,
> So early in the May-time,
> At the break o' the day! [p. 424]

The words of this ballad take us back to the relatively idyllic
scene of the May-walking, thereby emphasizing the incongruity between reality and Tess's fantasy. That they failed to
dance with one another years earlier at the May Day dance,
at "the break o' the day," foreshadows the fact that Tess and
Angel remain apart even while married.

In a recent study of *Far from the Madding Crowd*, Ellen-Monica
Gibb establishes a structural connection between that novel
and the traditional English ballad form. Gibb relies on Donald
Davidson's "The Traditional Basis of Thomas Hardy's Fiction," which asserts that the novelist characteristically imi-
tated the ballad structure in his fiction. In her essay, Gibb
presents several striking similarities between Hardy's fiction
and balladry: "the primary focus of attention on the narrative;
the single-stranded plots, which rarely ever double back to
fill in missing details; the balanced pairs of opposed characters; the sharp definition of scene and background; and the

face-to-face encounters of individuals with one another, which are the life of the tale and ballad and also the primary method of advancing action" ("Thomas Hardy's Use of Traditional English Ballad Form," pp. 187-88) "Gibb's argument is convincing and provides, by extension, a way of experiencing *Tess of the d'Urbervilles* in folkloristic terms and the characters as archetypal figures. As Gibb points out, "The *type* of action [in ballads] has mostly to do with the stuff of tabloid journalism: tales of lust, revenge, domestic crime, adultery, betrayal, and murder" (p. 188). *Tess* of course is about all of these and resembles a folk ballad tragedy in both form and subject matter.

Tess, "a pure woman," is presented by Hardy as the quintessential innocent country maiden. In the novel, we follow Tess's blind confrontations with fate; the leaping and lingering scenes of tragedy that compose her life resound with archetypal overtones. On several occasions Tess is compared to Eve in the Garden of Eden, while Angel is compared to Adam, and Alec is compared to the serpent. The initial meeting between Tess and Alec d'Urberville takes place in his garden, where he feeds her strawberries against her will:

> Selecting a specially fine product of the 'British Queen' variety, he stood up and held it by the stem to her mouth.
> "No—no!" she said quickly, putting her fingers between his hand and her lips. "I would rather take it in my own hand."
> "Nonsense!" he insisted; and in a slight distress she parted her lips and took it in. [p. 81]

"She obeyed like one in a dream" (p. 81), we are told. In his way, Alec asserts his power and Tess responds with innocence, and "thus the thing began" (p. 82). Immediately after the rape scene in The Chase, Tess walks home to Marlott and looks over her valley: "It was always beautiful from here; it was terribly beautiful to Tess to-day, for since her eyes last fell upon it she had learnt that the serpent hisses where the

sweet birds sing, and her views of life had been totally
changed for her by the lesson" (p. 123).[22] Later in the novel,
Tess leaves home for the second time, and as she is walking
along she sings several ballads, then sings a psalm that she
remembers from "a Sunday morning before she had eaten of
the tree of knowledge" (p. 158). And later, at Talbothays, just
before Angel asks Tess to marry him, we are told that she
regarded him "as Eve at her second waking might have regarded Adam" (p. 232).

Alec is clearly established as a demonic figure in the novel.
He is described as having "an almost swarthy complexion,
with full lips, badly moulded, though red and smooth, above
which was a well-groomed black moustache with curled
points. . . . Despite the touches of barbarism in his contours,
there was a singular force in the gentleman's face, and in his
bold rolling eye" (p. 79). Alec is said to have a low, cunning
laugh; he deceives Tess; he spies on her, tricks her, traps her,
and manipulates events in such a way that she becomes, finally, his possession. Furthermore, his complete obsession
with her results in his rejecting his call to preach, however
insincere that call.

A telling scene that reflects the demon-lover interaction
between Tess and Alec occurs in "Phase the Sixth: The Con-
vert." At Flintcomb-Ash Farm, when Alec, standing near the
threshing machine, tries to convince Tess to enter his "trap"
and go away with him, she suddenly strikes him with her
glove, drawing blood. " 'Now, punish me!' she said, turning
up her eyes to him with the hopeless defiance of the sparrow's
gaze before its captor twists its neck. 'Whip me, crush me,
you need not mind those people under the rick! I shall not
cry out. Once victim, always victim—that's the law!' " (p.
411).[23] Alec replies, " 'Remember, my lady, I was your master
once! I will be your master again. If you are any man's wife
you are mine! . . . You don't know me yet! But I know you' "
(p. 412). Again, we are told that Tess behaved "as one in a
dream" (p. 412).

A few days later, Alec returns to the threshing field in the
evening, at nightfall, the time of day "which in the frost of

winter comes as a fiend and the warmth of summer as a lover, [but] came as a tranquilizer on this March day" (p. 430), suggesting a state of numbness. In this state Tess encounters Alec, whose visage unmistakably resembles the devil's: "By-and-by he dug so close to her that the fire-beams were reflected as distinctly from the steel prongs of his fork as from her own. On going up to the fire to throw a pitch of dead weeds upon it, she found that he did the same on the other side. The fire flared up, and she beheld the face of d'Urberville" (p. 431). Alec then teases Tess by saying, "A jester might say this is just like Paradise. You are Eve, and I am the old Other One come to tempt you in the disguise of an inferior animal" (p. 431). Tess replies that she does not think of him as Satan, but of course the woman in "The Demon Lover" ballad also failed to recognize her lover as a demon until it was too late. In the end, Tess murders Alec to free herself of his hold over her and to return to Angel. Like all victims in demon-lover tales, Tess struggles against the annihilating force of her demon-lover, but ultimately Alec succeeds in destroying her, for she is hanged for her crime.

In the twentieth century, the demon-lover motif continues to be a primary structural vehicle through which many stories are told. D.H. Lawrence's "The Princess" and Elizabeth Bowen's "The Demon Lover" are twentieth-century demon-lover tales. To better comprehend these stories we need to explore ways in which the authors use the demon-lover motif. "The Princess" is a bizarre balladlike tale which depicts psychological and physical violence. Critics tend to view the story as rather dark, sardonic, and nihilistic. In *D.H. Lawrence*, George J. Becker states that the psychosexual violence is the most notable characteristic of the story (p. 120). Ronald Draper calls "The Princess" a compulsion tale (*D.H. Lawrence*). Unlike most of the other critics, however, Draper blames the victim in the tale, Dollie Urquhart, for what he considers her inevitable destruction, due to her selfishness and stubborn determination (p. 130).

Kingsley Widmer provides a comprehensive paradigm which illuminates the story for us beyond explanations provided by other Lawrence critics. In *The Art of Perversity*, Widmer identifies "the demon lover" as the hero—or rather the anti-hero—of many of Lawrence's short stories, including "The Princess."

Although Widmer does not mention "The Demon Lover" ballad to support his discussion of "The Princess," he does justify his interpretation by emphasizing Lawrence's use of a demon-lover to express an "inversion of public values" (p. 43). To explain his approach to Lawrence's demon-lover stories, Widmer says, "We need . . . some sense of the demonic tradition—as a prerequisite for accurately understanding Lawrence. Otherwise, willy-nilly, the reader will base his expectations, as have so many writers about Lawrence, on morality rather than amorality, order rather than rebellion, and on moderation rather than intensity. Or perhaps we may put it this way: the reader of Lawrence must recognize the nihilistic way to knowledge as the arcanum of the Lawrencean lover and hero" (p. 43). The critic's description of Lawrence's demon-lover figure seems very much like the demon-lovers in the old ballad and in the stories told by Brontë, Hardy, and others. Lawrence's demon-lover figure, Widmer writes, is a "dark hero . . . emphatically 'the outsider' . . . the rebel, the force of seduction and flame, mystery and darkness, passion and death . . . [and] the point of all dark heroes is that the world of passion must be alien to the domestic and social order. The intense desires connected with the deepest knowledge of sexuality and death reveal an ultimate chaos and the denial of all authority" (pp. 50-51). Other characters, Widmer states, view the demon-lover as a mysterious but dangerous intruder in their midst, capable of expressing both tenderness and rage.

To examine "The Princess" in the context of Widmer's description of demon-lover as protagonist (or antagonist) helps us to comprehend this obscure tale. As we have seen by looking at several versions of the ballad in chapter 3, the demon-lover motif involves a woman, her lover, a secret vow (except in fragments and corrupt texts), and the return of the lover, who comes to claim the woman in some way. Chaos and destruction result. Lawrence's plot deviates from the usual pattern in one important way. Rather than a story of an obsessed lover returning to regain control over a woman with whom he had exchanged vows, Lawrence ingeniously sets up parallel experiences with two men—two demon-lovers, in a sense—to whom the woman falls victim. The demon-lover experience, in this case, involves a revisitation of a powerfully destructive force.

In the story, Lawrence presents Colin Urquhart, Dollie's father, as an early demon-figure in his daughter's life. Colin is a "bit mad," and there is a strong suggestion that he is otherworldly and unreal. After three years of marriage Colin's wife Hannah "broke": "It was like living with a fascinating spectre. About most things he was completely, even ghostly oblivious . . . he just wasn't . . . all there . . . he was like a living echo! His very flesh, when you touched it, did not seem quite the flesh of a real man" (pp. 473-74).

Lawrence carefully establishes a psychological explanation for Dollie's subsequent behavior in the story. After her mother died when Dollie was two years old, her father taught her that she was different from other people: "My little Princess must never take too much notice of people and the things they say and do" (p. 475). In a crucial passage, Colin explains to her the essential difference that sets her apart from others:

> Inside everybody there is another creature, a demon which doesn't care at all. You peel away all the things they say and do and feel, as cook peels away the outside of the onions. And in the middle of everybody there is a green demon which you can't peel away. And this green demon never changes, . . . and this demon is a man's real self, and a woman's real self. It doesn't really care about anybody, it belongs to the demons and the primitive fairies, who never care. But, even so, there are big demons and mean demons, and splendid demonish fairies, and vulgar ones. But there are no royal fairy women left. Only you, my little Princess. You are the last of the royal race of the old people. . . . And that is why, darling, you will never care for any of the people

in the world very much. Because their demons are all
dwindled and vulgar. They are not royal. . . . Always
remember that. And always remember, it is a *great secret.*
[p. 475]

From the beginning of the story we see that Mary Henrietta
Urquhart—called Dollie by her mother and The Princess by
her father—has an elusive self-identity. "She seemed like a
changeling" (p. 476), we are told, suggesting that her identity
was provided by her father and frozen in time, not to be
altered: "She looked as if she had stepped out of a picture.
But no one, to her dying day, ever knew exactly the strange
picture her father had framed her in and from which she never
stepped" (p. 476).

Colin provides her with two major lessons about life: intimacy with anyone other than her father is impossible, and
"benevolent politeness" is the proper attitude that she should
adopt toward others (p. 476). The first lesson constitutes the
solemn vow typical of the demon-lover motif: "I am a prince,
and you a princess . . . And we keep our secret between us,
all alone" (p. 476). The second lesson results in Dollie's re-
sponding to people with condescension and impertinence,
which produces hatred in them. As perpetually un-self-aware
as she is, however, she "could never understand the volcanic
phallic rage with which coarse people could turn on her in a
paroxysm of hatred" (p. 478).

At the end of Colin's life, his madness intensifies and he
turns on Dollie with a violent rage which almost kills her. His
true self, then, is a demon-lover and Dollie is the victim. After
Colin dies, the narrator tells us, "She was the Princess, and
sardonically she looked out on a princeless world" (p. 479).
Dollie seems lost and empty of purpose after her father's
death, an "empty vessel in the enormous warehouse of the
world" (p. 480). In this state of mind she turns to the thought
of marriage "in the blank abstract" (p. 480) because she has
nothing better to do. Lawrence seems to imply a certain inevitable calamity of experience due to her lack of self-awareness and self-directedness. Dollie is psychically vulnerable.

In search of a husband, Dollie and her companion Miss

Cummins go to a ranch in New Mexico where Dollie meets Domingo Romero. Romero fits very well the physical description of a demon-lover: dressed entirely in black, he is "dark," "sinister," "different," "with a look of heavy meaninglessness, self-torture and death-worship about him common to Mexicans in that locality" (p. 482). In his black eyes there is "a spark in the midst of the blackness of static despair" (p. 483); it is this spark, Lawrence informs us, that sets him apart from others and attracts Dollie: "And instantly she knew that he was a gentleman, that his 'demon,' as her father would have said, was a fine demon. And instantly her manner towards him changed" (p. 483). Dollie recognizes a certain similarity between Romero and her father. In keeping with the demon-lover motif, the *essence* of destructive power returns in the form of Romero.

Romero treats Dollie with a "subtle, insidious male kindness she had never known before" (p. 484), and yet, "At the same time, curiously, he gave her the feeling that death was not far from him. Perhaps he *too* was half in love with death. However that may be, the sense she had that death was not far from him made him 'possible' to her" (p. 485; my emphasis). At this point in the story Lawrence seems to suggest that the events which follow are somehow determined by conditions that already exist within the hearts of Dollie and Romero. The key word in the above passage is "*too*": perhaps Romero is—as Dollie is—half in love with death. For Dollie, it was death which claimed her father, death which separates them, and death and destruction which finally seduce her.

When the idea of journeying into the mountains to search for wild animals occurs to Dollie, she pursues the plan with "an obstinacy characteristic of her nature, an obstinacy tinged perhaps with madness" (p. 487). She quickly becomes obsessed with a desire "to look over the mountains into their secret heart . . . to see the wild animals move about in their wild unconsciousness" (pp. 487-88).

As a victim, Dollie is similar to the woman in the ballad because she *pursues* danger; she actively participates in her demon-lover experience. The skillful way in which Lawrence relates the journey up the mountain reveals to us the dynamics of Dollie's fateful assent. The narrow, rocky trail leads, symbolically, up the shadowy, lee side of the mountain. On the way up the mountain, Dollie becomes noticeably less self-aware, less conscious of herself as a willful person capable of good judgment. Early in the journey she senses something corrupt but fails to relate it to herself in a realistic way: "And again the chill entered the Princess's heart as she realized what a tangle of decay and despair lay in the virgin forests" (p. 490). She continues up the mountain "not knowing what she felt" (p. 490). When Miss Cummins' horse goes lame Dollie feels so angry that "she was blind to everything else. . . . almost unconscious" (p. 493). Nevertheless, she rides on alone thinking of her "adventure": "She was going on along with Romero. But then she was very sure of herself, and Romero was not the kind of man to do anything to her against her will. This was her first thought" (p. 493).

Here Lawrence creates an expectation in us because, as readers, we see Romero more clearly than Dollie sees him. We know, for instance, that Romero had looked at Dollie with "a strange, demon-like watchfulness" (p. 490) on the trail, and we suspect that Romero may have selected the buckskin for Miss Cummins because he knew that the horse was not capable of enduring the rugged terrain.

Dollie's "fixed desire . . . to look into the inner chaos of the Rockies" (p. 493) drives her onward. When she reaches the foot of the summit she stops to wait for Romero. After he arrives Dollie seems more and more out of touch with herself and with reality. The incongruity of her clothes, of her lunch with the two Indians, of the "fairy-like gentleness" (p. 494) all around her does not penetrate her consciousness. Romero leads Dollie from her "little paradise" on the summit up "the stark corpse slope, among dead spruce, fallen and ash-grey, into the wind" (p. 496). The stark, dead landscape frightens Dollie: "And yet now one of her desires was fulfilled. She had seen it, the massive, gruesome, repellent core of the Rockies. . . . She had looked down into the intestinal knot of these mountains. She was frightened. She wanted to go back" (pp.

496-97). The terrifying core of the mountain represents the objective correlative of the demon self that she had witnessed in her father, and yet decisive action is impossible for her as she seems to negate herself, thus subjecting herself to Romero, giving him power over her as she had turned her will over to her father.

As they travel together, Dollie notices that Romero seems "strange and ominous, only the demon of himself" (p. 497). "She closed her eyes," Lawrence tells us, "and let her consciousness evaporate away" (pp. 497-98) as she moves "in blind, reckless pursuit" (p. 498) toward an unknown destination. By the time they finally arrive at the dilapidated cabin, Dollie is "in a sort of stupor" (p. 500) and Romero is "energetic and full of force" (p. 501). These descriptions of them are revealing, and during this scene Lawrence associates Dollie with ice, cold, and fear, while he associates Romero with fire, passion, and wildness. By this point in the story, Lawrence has established all of the preconditions which have, for Dollie and Romero, led to this situation. Dollie has suspended self-awareness in favor of psychological and moral numbness; Romero, however, is consistently dark, mysterious, ominous, and forceful.

The first night at the cabin when Dollie wakes from her dream of snow and death, she cannot quite identify what she wants. Lawrence seems to be reinforcing the idea that Dollie relinquishes responsibility for herself by being unaware, and that it is her unwillingness to remain in control of herself which makes her a victim. She wakes Romero because she is cold and wants him to make her warm: "And he was warm, but with a terrible animal warmth that seemed to annihilate her" (p. 504). At the moment of the sexual act, Lawrence interjects a key passage: "She had never, never wanted to be given over to this. But she had *willed* that it should happen to her. And according to her will, she lay and let it happen. But she never wanted it. She never wanted to be thus assailed and handled, and mauled. She wanted to keep herself to herself" (p. 504). Dollie rejects the possibility of intimacy because of her vow to her father. She rejects the stark reality of sexual contact, yet she certainly precipitates the event by her failure to assert her will. Dollie willed it to happen by allowing herself to be seduced by the dark, mysterious force of evil, by allowing that force to numb her.

In one sweeping symbolic gesture Romero throws Dollie's clothes into a nearly frozen pond, and in the ensuing chaos they are stripped to their essential selves: "They were like two demons watching one another. In his face, beyond a sort of unrelieved gloom, was a demonish desire for death" (p. 506). To conquer her he rapes her repeatedly. Dollie's ironic resistance comes too late: "I won't have anybody's will put over me. You can't succeed. Nobody could. You can never get me under your will" (p. 508). Despite Dollie's protests, however, her demon-lover succeeds in conquering her because she has effectively denied the reality of her dangerous predicament.

Critics of another modern tale of aggression and victimization, Elizabeth Bowen's "The Demon Lover," differ radically regarding her methods and her meaning. Allan E. Austin says in *Elizabeth Bowen*, " 'The Demon Lover' is a ghost story which builds up then culminates like an Alfred Hitchcock movie" (p. 117). In "Cracks in the Psyche: Elizabeth Bowen's 'The Demon Lover,' " Douglas A. Hughes refutes Austin's interpretation: "Far from being a supernatural story, 'The Demon Lover' is a masterful dramatization of acute psychological delusion, of the culmination of paranoia in a time of war" (p. 411). According to Hughes, when Kathleen Drover returns to her old, abandoned house, she is so overcome by an "irrational guilt she feels for betraying her lover" (p. 412) that she hallucinates and in the taxi "passes into madness" (p. 413). Daniel V. Fraustino disagrees with Hughes' interpretation of the story. In "Elizabeth Bowen's 'The Demon Lover': Psychosis or Seduction?," Fraustino suggests that Hughes exaggerates Kathleen's emotional instability and that Bowen carefully establishes her protagonist's lucidity. He further proposes that the empty house reminds Kathleen of "her impoverished married life" (p. 484) which leads to a "growing unconscious need to escape" (p. 485). Fraustino concludes that the soldier has actually returned to kill Kathleen. Comparing Bowen's story with Scott's version of the ballad, Fraustino says, "As in the ballad, the fiancé has returned (importantly he was only 'presumed dead') to claim his lover-victim on their silver anniversary. In Bowen's story, however, he is a psychopath, not the devil" (p. 486).

In the earliest version of the ballad the returning lover is a "spirit in the night," and although in her story Bowen skillfully balances the probable with the improbable, she provides subtle clues so we may decipher this enigmatic tale. "The Demon Lover" seems, however, neither a ghost story nor a story of Kathleen Drover's madness. Fraustino's suggestion that the soldier does in fact return for Kathleen twenty-five years after she "Plighted . . . [her] sinister troth" (Bowen, *Collected*, p. 664) seems reasonable. As Fraustino points out, the soldier was only presumed dead, and thus he returns at the "hour arranged." Fraustino, however, fails to comment on Bowen's use of the demon-lover motif as a means of expressing collective and private devastation.

It is clear from the story that Kathleen Drover and her family had lived in the house until London was bombed, which means that they must have moved sometime after September 7, 1940, the date of the first London blitz. We also know from the story that during the last week in August 1941, less than a year after having moved to the country, Kathleen returns to her abandoned home to gather some things left there by her family.

When she enters the house and finds a letter written to her by a soldier she had known twenty-five years earlier, a man believed to have died in World War I, it is significant that she immediately thinks of the part-time caretaker who has looked after the house during the time it has stood empty. Regarding the caretaker, Bowen tells us, Kathleen "was never sure that she trusted him" (p. 661). The letter makes Kathleen feel intruded upon—and by "someone contemptuous of her ways" (p. 662). Little by little we become acutely aware of Kathleen's dilemma: the caretaker has the only other key to the house and he is supposedly out of town; a man who is presumably dead has written her a letter stating that he will meet her "at the hour arranged" (p. 662).

For Kathleen, the letter evokes a series of memories about the soldier she met when she was nineteen years old. He was on leave, and after knowing him for only one week she became engaged to him. Kathleen remembers the power he had had over her and the "unnatural promise" (p. 663) she had made to him, the promise referred to in the letter: "In view of the fact that nothing has changed, I shall rely upon you to keep your promise" (p. 662). In many versions of the ballad, the woman and her lover had exchanged vows in the past, and when the lover returns, the woman acquiesces and follows her former lover. In Bowen's story, however, Kathleen becomes more terrified as the story proceeds.

The letter becomes a kind of bridge between the past and the present for Kathleen as she distinctly recalls the circumstances under which she had made her fateful promise. She remembers "the complete suspension of *her* existence" (p. 665) twenty-five years earlier and the sense of disconnectedness which followed: "She already felt that unnatural promise drive down between her and the rest of all human kind. No other way of having given herself could have made her feel so apart, lost and forsworn" (pp. 663-64). She remembers that he was not kind to her and that he was obsessed with her: "Mother said he never considered me. He was set on me; that was what it was— not love" (p. 665). When she tries to remember his face she finds that she cannot; moreover, she cannot remember ever having seen it completely: "So, wherever he may be waiting, I shall not know him. You have no time to run from a face you do not expect" (p. 665). Bowen carefully attributes the characteristics of a demon-lover to the soldier, characteristics consistent with those found in the old ballad: power, mystery, cruelty, and obsession. The terror for Kathleen is the uncertainty of the situation combined with the potential for evil.

Twenty-five years earlier she had managed to escape the unnatural hold the soldier had on her: "[S]he caught a breath for the moment when she could go running back there into the safe arms of her mother and sister. . . . Only a little more than a minute later she was free" (p. 663). At the end of the story when Kathleen escapes from the house she senses that someone else leaves the basement at the same moment. As she climbs into the taxi which "appeared already to be alertly waiting for her" (p. 666), the clock strikes seven—their "appointed hour." Surprised by the taxi's "knowing movements," Kathleen taps on the glass to get the driver's attention: "The driver braked to what was almost a stop, turned round and slid the glass panel back: the jolt of this flung Mrs. Drover forward till her face was almost into the glass" (p. 666). To explain this curious ending to the story, Hughes suggests that when the clock strikes seven Kathleen becomes immediately convinced that "her hour has come and she takes the *unsuspecting* taxi driver for a fiend" (Hughes, p. 413, my emphasis) and that at this moment Kathleen "passes into madness." Close reading of the text, however, reveals no discomfort over the sound of the clock; on the contrary, Kathleen thinks that the taxi is her refuge until the driver turns the corner.

Fraustino correctly refers to the old ballad "The Demon Lover" as proof that Kathleen's absent lover has actually returned to claim her (p. 487). Building on Fraustino's theory, it is crucial to realize that when the taxi driver turns around, Kathleen's jolt is a jolt of recognition: she sees before her the caretaker whom she suddenly recognizes as the soldier-lover from her past. Bowen provides several hints which support this contention. When Kathleen married William Drover several years earlier and they subsequently moved into this same house, Kathleen felt that she was being watched (p. 664). The caretaker, we are told, has the only other key to the house, and at the same moment Kathleen leaves the house someone else, Bowen hints, quietly lets himself out as well. This reading of the ending implies deliberate deception over time, thus increasing the irony of Bowen's tale.

In keeping with the early ballad, Kathleen's demon-lover carries her off into the night, into "the hinterland." In Bowen's tale, however, the revenant lover stalks the woman, terrorizes her, and abducts her. Significantly, Bowen's demon-lover tale takes place in war-ravaged London. Kathleen's return to the city produces in her a psychic vulnerability, leaving her exposed to evil influences and personal devastation. War causes, as Hughes points out, "cracks in the psyche." The soldier Kathleen met during World War I took advantage of her vulnerability, extracted an "unnatural promise" from her, and then pursues her during World War II to terrify, to destroy, to annihilate her.

Bowen brilliantly uses the demon-lover motif to expose the rape of war, the disruption of society, and the incomprehensibility of personal tragedy. The plot recreates the kind of psychological disconnectedness that war causes—the terror, the uncertainty, the denied reality, the disappearance of people, and the death. In the "Preface" to the American edition of *The Demon Lover*, Bowen discusses the psychological milieu in England during World War II: "It seems to me that during the war in England the overcharged sub-consciousnesses of everybody overflowed and merged. . . . What was happening was out of all proportion to our faculties for knowing, thinking and checking up. . . . There was an element of chanciness and savageness about everything" (cited in *Collected Impressions*, pp. 48-50). By calling her story "The Demon Lover," Bowen creates a contemporary demon-lover "ballad" to express fears during a time when the people of England felt victimized and vulnerable. Unlike the ghostly lover in the oldest version of the ballad and the demon with the cloven foot in Scott's version, the demon-lover in Bowen's tale is an actual person who stalks his victim relentlessly and mercilessly—and that is the horror of it. The demon in this story personifies unremitting evil in an otherwise civilized world.

In Bowen's story as in the ballad, the victim and the demon-lover disappear into the night, while in Lawrence's story they negate each other, which results in psychological annihilation. By the end of the story Romero, who is by then clearly bent on self-destruction, is killed, while Dollie survives, though "slightly crazy" (Lawrence, *Stories*, p. 512). While Bowen uses the demon-lover motif to express a collective, unconscious fear of overpowering evil *within* civilized society, Brontë, Hardy, and Lawrence concentrate on the psychological dynamics relating to evil which take place on the fringe of civilization. As in "The Demon Lover" ballad, Lawrence's demon-figure carries his victim off to "the mountain of hell," where savageness and destruction occur. In his modern demon-lover tale, Lawrence demonstrates a causal relationship by adapting the ballad to show preexisting factors: in "The Princess," Colin predisposes Dollie to evil influences by inhibiting her will and by disorienting her; when Romero comes into Dollie's life (like the Prince of Darkness) she is easily seduced, and when he attempts to conquer her, she cannot effectively and willfully resist.

All of these authors—Brontë, Hardy, Lawrence, and Bowen—recreate the demon-lover motif through their fiction. To varying degrees, these demon-lover tales have the twofold quality of demonism and blindness, or obsession and victimization. The demon-lovers all resemble one another in both physical characteristics and personality traits. They are all conniving, manipulative, deceptive, and obsessed—qualities associated historically with the demonic. The victims of these stories share three major characteristics: blindness regarding the demon-lover, suspended awareness, and willingness to become a victim.

To come to terms with the demon-lover motif as a pervasive psychic image, we must explore questions relating to motivation. The concluding chapter seeks to uncover why certain men, as represented by myths, ballads, and literary works, become demon-lovers, why they become pathologically obsessed with women in such a way that they ultimately destroy the others' freedom, will, health, or life. The next chapter also seeks to identify psychological explanations that underlie the role of victim assumed by the women in the works discussed above. By exposing the psychological dynamics involved in pathological aggression and pathological victimization, we are better able to account for the widespread popularity of the demon-lover motif as a primary psychic image in the collective unconscious.

# FIVE

## Demon-Lovers
## and Their Victims

> There are a thousand hacking at the branches of evil
> to one who is striking at the root.
>
> HENRY DAVID THOREAU

"The Demon Lover" ballad provides a stark view of a particular aggressor/victim relationship that has been widely expressed throughout literary history. The demon-lover conflict expressed in skeletal form by the ballad may be traced from Greek mythology through the Old and New Testaments and strongly resembles the accounts by "witches" of their alleged encounters with Satan from the eleventh through the seventeenth centuries. The demon-lover motif runs through many of the ballads and tales of Britain and is echoed in works of fiction by major writers from Richardson to D.H. Lawrence. The tradition continues in contemporary literature as well, including popular romance novels. Despite the pervasiveness of the demon-lover motif, critics have largely ignored the similarities among stories, myths, and songs that exhibit the dynamics simplified by the ballad.

Folk ballads, of course, are more impersonal than formal literature and thus are more capable of simplifying motivation. In contrast to elaborate fictional worlds created by writers such as Emily Brontë, Bram Stoker, or Thomas Hardy, "The Demon Lover" ballad is a distilled version of the writers' observations about destructive human relationships. Compared with fully realized works of fiction, ballads seem very dreamlike: in the sense that unlikely events happen, the rhythm and repetition of the songs themselves make the stories told seem removed from reality, and commonplaces function in ballads like symbolic props from our own lives that reappear in our dreams. Ballads serve a purpose similar to the way dreams affect our waking lives; i.e., they reduce experience to its simplest terms, however abstract or cryptic. "The Demon Lower" ballad simplifies a particular type of human conflict in a mythical fashion, a conflict "washed" through centuries of oral and written balladry, while the fiction that repeats the same basic plot formula makes the conflict noticeably more complex. Fiction writers present more sophisticated views of the demon-lover conflict because they hope to capture the intricacies that ballads are not equipped to handle.

Jung has pointed out the similarity between dreams and myths, further suggesting that because poetry often relies on myths there is a connection between dreams and poetry, or in this case, ballads. The demon-lover figures that appear in myths, literature, folklore, dreams, and dreamlike experiences (incubus encounters) all have, as has previously been established, certain qualities in common. In "Jungian Psychology and Its Uses in Folklore," Carlos C. Drake comments on the connection between dreams and folklore, suggesting that archetypes may be found in both: "In myths and folktales it is often possible to spot shadow figures and situations similar to those found in dreams and fantasies but which, as mentioned, are devoid of any personal detail" (p. 126). The demon-lover motif, then, appears to be a spontaneous, primordial reflection of the uncensored psyche, expressed idiosyncratically by artists and dreamers.

Along with Freud, Jung believed that a personal unconscious is formed during an individual's lifetime but, unlike Freud, he also believed in "the collective unconscious." The archetypes contained in the collective unconscious present themselves to the conscious mind from time to time and influence personality, according to Jung, who sees the act of becoming aware of these images as a significant moral achievement. One of the more influential archetypes, disturbing to encounter in oneself, is what he refers to as "the shadow." Human beings, he proposes, incorporate two distinctly different sets of attributes, one positive and the other negative, represented in their extreme as love and hate. Essentially, the shadow is the negative, destructive, and instinctive side of human nature.

As the shadow self is, understandably, difficult to accept, it tends to be extremely well controlled; hence, Jung contends, in most people the shadow remains unassimilated into the personality. Instead of integrating both sides of ourselves, Jung theorizes that we *project* our own negative qualities onto others in order to express parts of ourselves that would otherwise seem too dangerous. Projections of this type are so emotionally charged that it is difficult to recognize the source of our own projected fears, hatred, and violence. Jung, in fact, refers to this shadow as a "demon," "a raging monster," "a beast" (*Two Essays on Analytical Psychology*, p. 30). Explaining the dynamics of projection, he states: "[W]hen somebody projects the devil upon his neighbor, he does so because this person has something about him which makes the attachment of such an image possible. But this is not to say that the man is on that account a devil. . . . Nor need the projector necessarily be a devil, although he has to recognize that he has something just as devilish in himself, and has only stumbled upon it by projecting it" (*Essays*, p. 96).

Commenting on the task of the artist, Jung believes that the creative process involves an "unconscious animation of the archetype" (*Contributions to Analytical Psychology*, p. 248). The artist, in other words, brings to life primordial images with which we may identify, images that are very often most suppressed by contemporary society. "Therein lies the social importance of art," Jung writes; "it is constantly at work educating the spirit of the age, since it brings to birth those forms in which the age is most lacking" (*Contributions*, p. 248). When archetypes (the shadow, for instance) are collectively suppressed, they resurface in the images created by artists who "instinctively" seek to restore the psychic balance (*Spirit*, p. 104). According to Jung, artists create *projections* of the shadow as well as other archetypes that are causing tension in the collective unconscious, much as an individual might project troublesome emotions onto a neighbor. To understand art, he suggests, we must allow the experience of art to shape us as it shaped the artist; through this method of psychic identification, which Jung calls the "participation mystique," we may reconnect momentarily with the collective unconscious (*Spirit*, p. 105).

As I have suggested earlier, Jung's theory of the collective unconscious provides an explanation for the repetition of certain motifs that occur throughout literary history. The demon-lover motif under consideration in this study corresponds very well to "the shadow" that, according to Jung, tends to be deeply suppressed in individuals. Suppressed archetypes, he tells us, resurface in the form of art. Folklore scholars have tried for years to explain how ballads, tales, legends, superstitions, and so forth have been transmitted from generation to generation and from place to place. Yet theories of the oral transmission of folklore, an established principle, fail to account for the *interest* among the folk in certain stories, certain motifs. Theories postulated by Jung, however, suggest that certain motifs recur because of a collective repression of negative and destructive forces. In other words, artists express fears hidden or denied by their communities; members of those communities respond psychically, to use Jung's term, and emotionally to images that they cannot comprehend on a conscious level. Ballads, for example, that originated in the Renaissance have been perpetuated throughout the centuries because people have identified with the stories told by activating their "participation mystigue."

"The Demon Lover" tells the story of a vengeful lover who returns to punish his betrothed because she has been unfaithful. From another point of view, it is also the story of a woman who kisses her children goodbye and rushes toward her own destruction, learning too late the true nature of her demonic lover. The struggle depicted in the ballad and repeated endlessly throughout literature is the ontological conflict between what Jung calls the *animus* and the *anima*.[24] Briefly, the *animus* and the *anima* are the masculine and feminine qualities, respectively, of the psyche; Jung associates the word "Logos" with the *animus* and "Eros" with the *anima*. In general, Jung tells us, men tend to repress their "feminine" sides, yet project the *anima* outside of themselves onto women, while women project their own repressed *animus* in the same way onto men. The "anima/animus relationship is always full of 'animosity' " (*Aion*, p. 16), Jung states, which suggests that any interaction between *anima* and *animus* is bound to be one of conflict.

In the ballad, the returning lover stalks his victim, manipulates her through guilt ("I might have had a king's daughter"), and persuades her to run away with him by pretending to have considerable wealth; in short, he manifests the qualities of the *animus*—calculating logic, action, and power—and he also behaves aggressively, exhibiting a dangerous passion. The victim in the ballad manifests the qualities associated with the *anima*: emotionalism, passivity, and powerlessness; she demonstrates these traits by being easily swayed, by crying aboard ship when she misses her children, and by her inability to save herself. But she also calculates her reward for running off with her demon-lover and agrees to go with him only after he promises her riches and travel to exotic places. From the point of view of the collective human psyche, the demon-lover and his victim project the existence of one another: he represents negative masculinity and she represents negative femininity. Whenever a woman relies on her *animus*, as does the woman in the ballad, the man often resorts to seduction or rape, Jung asserts, as a way of exerting power over her (*Aion*, p. 15). In Jungian terms, the demon-lover projects his *anima* onto the woman, and because she expresses her *animus* as well, he destroys her.

As archetypes, the shadow, the *animus*, and the *anima* represent deep-seated images stored in the human psyche. The *animus* and the *anima* cannot be apprehended directly, according to Jung, but may be recognized as projections outside of oneself by those with great moral courage. The shadow archetype is more accessible to the conscious mind as one identifies one's own projections as mirror images of the self. "The Demon Lover" ballad presents metaphorically the dynamics of the human psyche; when the *animus* and *anima* join together following separation, conflict often results.

When the victim in the ballad (the *anima*) opposes her demon-lover (the *animus*) by insisting on returning to her children, she is ultimately destroyed. The earliest written version of the ballad, a British broadside issued during the late 1600s, is known by a long title which begins, "A Warning for Married Women." Historically, the ballad symbolically reinforced personal and social constraints placed upon women throughout history. The demon-lover motif has recurred through the ages because it demonstrates the power of men as well as the powerlessness of women and serves as a warning to women who would assert themselves and exhibit their capacity for rational action.

Balladeers express psychic dramas in their ballads, dramas which resemble those of the gods and goddesses of mythology, though on a smaller scale. The early balladeers were "merely deputies of the public voice," as ballad scholar Albert B. Friedman puts it (p. 61). And in the same way, novelists who duplicate the ballad's plot formula are engaged, along with the balladeers, in the act of "educating the spirit of the age," to repeat Jung's phrase.

Jung's theory regarding the activities of the psyche suggests that a human fascination with the demon-lover motif as it appears in the ballad and in various works of literature compels both artists and audience to project feelings of hatred and revenge as well as a fear of victimization onto objective, safe pieces of art for the sake of psychic balance. Ballads express archetypes that tend to be repressed by the collective unconscious. As listeners, we respond to stories told in old ballads because we intuitively wish to complete ourselves through a process that Jung calls "individuation." In other words, we have a drive to confront our "shadows" in the art with which we identify, and in the same way, artists project their shadows when they create art.

Speculations about underlying motivation for the often

shocking, often demonic aggression that takes place not only in the ballad but also in many works of fiction necessitates theorizing about the nature of madness and the nature of evil. This is especially true if we accept Jung's contention that within each of us is stored in the unconscious the collective experiences of the human race. To reclaim the part of consciousness that tends to be projected, according to Jung's theory, entails uncovering the fundamental motivations regarding destructive behavior perpetrated by demon-lover figures as well as the motivations of women who acquiesce or who are forced into the position of being victimized by their demon-lovers.

The pattern of interaction between the demon-lovers and their victims is discussed in more detail in chapters 2 and 4. But reiterating briefly the plot formula isolated in the ballad helps to establish the parallels between the folkloric renditions and full-fledged literary expressions of the motif. Stated in the motif's lowest common denominator, the demon-lover is an absent or revenant lover who returns to reestablish his claim on a woman, who subsequently falls victim to his destructive, vengeful behavior; the woman foolishly agrees to accompany her smooth-talking lover away from society and toward the isolation of the sea or the wilderness where he destroys her.

In *Wuthering Heights*, Heathcliff, a powerful character richly imbued with Satanic associations, is the embodiment of chaos and destruction for everyone with whom he comes into contact, including Catherine, for he seems demonically obsessed with her. After he leaves Catherine and returns to reestablish ties with her, it becomes clear that Heathcliff's intent is to destroy Catherine by absorbing her, by possessing her as he comes closest to doing during their final scene together the night she dies. His revenge is precipitated by Catherine's disloyalty when she announces to Nelly her decision to marry Edgar Linton. Similarly, in several versions of the ballad the returning lover attributes his revenge to the unfaithfulness of the woman. Catherine continues to seek Heathcliff's company throughout the novel, subjecting herself to his destructive

influence in the same way that the victim in the ballad abdicates responsible action in favor of danger, mystery, and
the unknown, all of which are personified by her demon-
lover.

*Wuthering Heights* deviates from the plot formula found in
the ballad in one important way. Catherine identifies so completely with Heathcliff ("I *am* Heathcliff") that she becomes
his demon-lover, too, in a sense, as they become mutually
destructive. In Brontë's novel, the demon-lover conflict extends beyond the grave as Catherine's ghost apparently returns to haunt and torment Heathcliff, as he, meanwhile,
tortures her *in absentia* through Isabella, Cathy, Linton, and
others who remind him of his separation from the object of
his obsession.

Thomas Hardy creates an archetypal demon-lover conflict
in *Tess of the d'Urbervilles* when he pits the deceitful, obsessed
Alec d'Urberville against the vulnerable, "pure" Tess. Many
critics believe that Alec rapes Tess in the Chase, that he com-
mits a violent act that specifically victimizes women.[25] Following her defilement, however, Tess, true to the plot formula
of the ballad, freely takes up the role of victim by returning
to Alec, her demon-lover. Ultimately, however, Alec and Tess
destroy one another—Alec by obsessively controlling Tess
and subduing her will, and Tess by murdering Alec to assure
her escape, an act which subsequently leads to her execution.

The demon-lover conflict in D.H. Lawrence's "The Princess," deviates somewhat from the dynamics depicted in the
ballad as the destructive influence of Dollie's father predisposes her to a demon-lover involvement. However, Romero's
obsession and his urge to destroy, as well as Dollie's lack of
self-awareness and perception, combine to duplicate the plot
formula found in "The Demon Lover." In this story Romero
repeatedly rapes his victim, which is of course his way of
conquering her, of overpowering her will. Like the victim in
the ballad, Dollie freely agrees to being carried off to the wilderness where harm comes to her.

Elizabeth Bowen's "The Demon Lover" seems more a distilled literary representation of the demon-lover motif than

the other literary works under consideration. Clearly, Bowen intends for us to make a direct connection to the old ballad as the revenant lover in the story, a soldier, returns to a deserted, bombed out part of London to claim the woman to whom he was once engaged, just as the sailor returns for his victim in the ballad. Unlike the woman in the ballad, however, Kathleen Drover does not freely choose to accompany her demon-lover into the wilderness; instead, she falls victim to her own lack of perception, as do all of the other women who are victimized by demon-lovers. Just as the woman in the ballad seals her own destruction when she fails to perceive her companion's cloven feet and thus the danger she is in, Mrs. Drover fails to rely on her intuition, fails to acknowledge the danger and terror of her predicament, and fails to discern her own life-preserving choices, Instead, like all other victims of demon-lovers, she moves entranced toward her demise and is finally carried off into the night, into the wilderness, against her will.

Many other works of British fiction contain features of the demon-lover motif, such as Charlotte Brontë's *Jane Eyre*; Doris Lessing's *The Four-Gated City*; numerous works by D.H. Lawrence, including "The Fox," *The Virgin and the Gipsy*, and *Women in Love*; and John Fowles's *The Collector* and *The French Lieutenant's Woman*. The motif appears in American fiction in Joyce Carol Oates's "Where Are You Going, Where Have You Been" (a short story made into the film *Smooth Talk*), Eudora Welty's "Robber Bridegroom," Willa Cather's *Lucy Gayheart*, William Styron's *Sophie's Choice*, and other works by leading contemporary writers. The scope of the present study prohibits further exploration of American works that were directly or indirectly influenced by the plot formula found in "The Demon Lover" ballad, although such a study is justified.

Demon-lover stories are currently in vogue, as the number and popularity of commercial films on the subject testify. Many film versions of *Dracula* have been made over the years, as Stoker's work remains one of the most popular stories ever told. Two cinematic versions of *Wuthering Heights* have been made, and *Tess of the d'Urbervilles* was also made into a film;

as films, *The French Lieutenant's Woman* and *Sophie's Choice* both received critical acclaim and were reasonably successful at the box office. The British film *Dance With a Stranger* reveals a stark, sadomasochistic relationship remarkable and terrifying for the never-ending pattern of aggression and victimization engaged in by the demon-lover figure, David Blakely, and his victim, Ruth Ellis. Their relationship resembles those of Heathcliff and Catherine, and Alec and Tess, as Ruth in time becomes victimizer as well. They are, then, enmeshed in a cycle of cruelty and victimization from which they escape only when Ruth murders David at the end of the film, a solution reminiscent of Tess's. The film is based on a true story. *Dance With a Stranger*, then, raises the demon-lover conflict out of the mythological realm and places it squarely in contemporary society where, many psychologists insist, the drama is played out every day.[26]

In *Loving with a Vengeance: Mass-Produced Fantasies for Women*, Tania Modleski explores what is essentially the same demon-lover motif discussed in this study by identifying the qualities of villains and victims that appear in Harlequin Romances, Gothic novels, and soap operas. All three genres, according to Modleski, include rakes who become obsessed with young, innocent women who, because of their purity, resist the advances of their would-be lovers. There is a strong emphasis in these works on violence and sexual passion, and the plots, according to Modleski, tend to revolve around conflicts initiated by the men's sexual advances. Modleski believes that these works have remained popular, especially with women, because they serve a cathartic function: "One of the great attractions of the rake was that he seemed to provide an exciting alternative to the staid domestic 'pleasures' which were all [that] good women were supposed to want" (p. 19). She further surmises that works (such as *Clarissa*) depicting the demon-lover motif have elevated women's self-image because the men in these novels spend a great deal of time " 'plotting the seductions' of the heroines" (p. 18). In many of these works, the heroines remain virtuous and succeed in winning over the rakes, who are converted by the women's purity and goodness. Thus, Modleski concludes, Harlequin Romances, Gothic novels, and soap operas, especially those written by women, often empower women, for the heroines sometimes are not defeated. Authors of Harlequin Romances, who follow a prescribed formula, must somehow explain the cruelty of the male lovers; this requirement of course differs from the demon-lover motif as crystallized by the ballad, for explanations are seldom provided for the aggression and brutality of demon-lovers.

The demon-lover stories discussed in chapter 4 are more akin to Gothic works than to Harlequin Romances. Distinguishing between these two genres, Modleski suggests, "Another way of expressing the difference between the two types of narrative is to say that the Harlequin heroine's feelings undergo a transformation from fear into love, whereas for the Gothic heroine, the transformation is from love into fear" (p. 60). The victims in demon-lover stories undergo a transformation from attraction to terror. They are not ultimately empowered by their demon-lover encounters; instead, they weaken and are defeated. Among the works explored in the present study, a significant exception is *Wuthering Heights*, as Catherine fails to be intimidated by Heathcliff. Catherine remains relatively strong in the face of Heathcliff's extreme possessiveness and inordinate desire to absorb her identity. At first glance, it seems that Thomas Hardy empowers Tess by having her murder Alec, but the final irony of the novel lies in the fact that Tess's liberation is illusory, a Pyrrhic victory, as she is executed in the end for her crime. In "The Princess," Dollie survives her nightmarish ordeal but is "slightly crazy" for the rest of her life. Kathleen Drover is carried off into "the hinterland" against her will and is thereby firmly defeated. Some women authors empower their female characters while others do not; Bowen, for example, follows the underlying structure of the ballad so closely that she must end her tale with Kathleen's defeat if she is to maintain a folkloric quality.

The underlying demon-lover conflict is succinctly expressed in Doris Lessing's *The Four-Gated City* during a confusing power play between Martha and her occasional lover

Jack: "It was like an endurance test. On her side: *How much can I stand?* On his: *How much can I get her to stand?*" (p. 403). This passage captures the conflict brought to life by demon-lover interactions as seen in the ballad as well as in the literature explored in chapter 4: the demon-lover typically crushes his victim's will, annihilates her sense of self-preservation, and ultimately oppresses her somehow. But why does the lover feel compelled to destroy the woman? And why doesn't the woman refuse to become a victim?

These two central questions regarding underlying motivation are critical if we are to come to an understanding of why the demon-lover motif is as prevalent as it is in nineteenth- and twentieth-century fiction. Human aggression has been the subject of interest and speculation among psychologists, philosophers, and theologians for centuries. Historically, religious sects have frequently been differentiated according to their beliefs concerning aggression or human destructiveness (e.g., Quakers, Muslims, Irish Catholics, and Irish Protestants). Contemporary thinkers often attribute the widespread violence that seems to describe modern society to a failure to love. In *Love and Will*, Rollo May tackles the question of aggression, concluding that violence is the inevitable result of profound alienation and powerlessness. Confusion about love and an inability to assert one's will, May suggests, are symptomatic of a contemporary, collective neurosis:

> The striking thing about love and will in our day is that, whereas in the past they were always held up to us as the *answer* to life's predicaments, they have now themselves become the *problem*. It is always true that love and will become more difficult in a transitional age; and ours is an era of radical transition. The old myths and symbols by which we oriented ourselves are gone, anxiety is rampant; we cling to each other and try to persuade ourselves that what we feel is love; we do not will because we are afraid that if we choose one thing or one person we'll lose the other, and we are too insecure to

take that chance. . . . The individual is forced to turn
inward; he becomes obsessed with the new form of the
problem of identity, namely Even-if-I-know-who-I-am,
I-have-no-significance. I am unable to influence others.
The next step is apathy. And the step following that is
violence. For no human being can stand the perpetually
numbing experience of his own powerlessness. [pp. 13-
14]

Human aggression as depicted by the demon-lover motif has
been present in folklore and literature over several centuries,
which suggests that every age is in some way an age of tran-
sition, and that change is so difficult for human beings, that
in response to anxiety regarding the unknown future, we tend
to behave in violent, self-destructive, and self-alienating
ways.

The demon-lover motif involves a struggle of wills: the
demon-lover in effect conquers the will of his victim through
deception and brute force; the victim fails to assert her will
and instead abdicates responsibility for herself in favor of self-
obliteration. Demon-lover interactions result in conquest
because of the particular dynamics that occur between the
victimizer and the victim: the demon-lover seeks to destroy
another's will, another's spirit, while the victim falls into his
hands by remaining unaware and by denying the reality of
her dangerous situation.

Freud theorized that human beings are guided by two in-
ternal forces, two instincts which he called the "life instinct"
and the "death instinct." These instincts or passions, he
states, are the drive to love and the drive to destroy. In *The
Anatomy of Human Destructiveness*, Erich Fromm expands
Freud's basic theory by differentiating between instincts and
character: "I shall try to show that character is man's 'second
nature,' the substitute for his poorly developed instincts; furthermore that the human passions (such as the striving for
love, tenderness, freedom as well as the lust for destruction,
sadism, masochism, the craving for power and property) are
answers to 'existential needs,' which in turn are rooted in the

very conditions of human existence. To put it briefly, *instincts* are answers to man's *physiological* needs, man's character-conditioned *passions* are answers to his *existential* needs and they are specifically human" (p. 26). Fromm goes on to say that human beings have extremely complex needs which, if met, give life meaning, and if frustrated, make us miserable enough to become destructive, According to Fromm, these needs "form the basis for man's interest in life, his enthusiasm, his excitement; they are the stuff from which not only his dreams are made but art, religion, myth, drama—all that makes life worth living" (p. 29). And when these needs are not met, "he creates for himself the drama of destruction" (p. 29). To Fromm, human destructiveness in the form of cruelty, crimes such as theft or rape, and war stem from an unfulfilled basic urge to apprehend meaning or the purpose of life. Without creativity to give life a purpose and a direction, Fromm implies, human beings turn naturally to destructive behavior as a way of coping with emptiness and absurdity.

The demon-lover tales identified in this study lend support to Fromm's contention that lack of meaning leads to violence. Lovelace, Alec d'Urberville, and Romero—three men whose morality demands close scrutiny—exemplify violence against women perpetrated in the form of rape, an act which is clearly a means of objectifying, subjugating, and humiliating women. As established in chapter 4, the demon-lover motif involves a confluence of energies relating to sexuality and death or destruction. Elizabeth Hardwick suggests in *Seduction and Betrayal: Women and Literature* that as an archetype a seducer must be an exaggerated, larger-than-life figure; in him there must be "something complicated and tangled and mysteriously compelling about a nature that has come to define itself through the mere fact of sex" (p. 185). Rollo May contends that men are sexually aggressive in order to compensate for their innermost fears of impotence (p. 106). Commenting on rape as an act of aggression, Susan Brownmiller states in *Against Our Will: Men, Women and Rape*: "Man's discovery that his genitalia could serve as a weapon to generate fear must rank as one of the most important discoveries of prehistoric times, along with the use of fire and the first crude stone axe. From prehistoric times to the present, I believe, rape has played a critical function. It is nothing more or less than a conscious process of intimidation by which *all men* keep *all women* in a state of fear" (p. 5). Brownmiller sees rape as a primordial, paradigmatic act of violence stemming from a fundamental fear of inadequacy.

Some of the acts committed by demon-lover figures found in both folk and formal literature are horrifying because of the unprovoked and inexplicable nature of the attacks as well as the suddenness, very often, with which women are victimized. Paul J. Stern provides a character analysis of what he calls "the absurd criminal" in his work *In Praise of Madness: Realness Therapy—The Self Reclaimed*. The "absurd" criminal or habitual victimizer, according to Stern, typically was victimized early in life by those he most depended upon and turned to for love and comfort—his parents, in most cases. Because he could not psychologically afford to be angry and outraged at them, he denied his feelings of rage and shifted those feelings to safe targets; he was "thus reduced to lashing out—if at all—blindly, impulsively, and inanely against substitutes who had no real meaning in his life" (p. 66). The absurd criminal looks *absurd*, according to Stern, because his fury is displaced. Furthermore, Stern points out that some people are completely "walled in by . . . unreality" (p. 61) and that to prove to themselves that they are real, they commit gratuitous acts of violence.

Emily Brontë provides enough background information about Heathcliff's childhood to conclude that he fits Stern's theory regarding the "absurd criminal" remarkably well. Much of Heathcliff's violent behavior is clearly displaced and gratuitous (e.g., his hanging of Isabella's dog). Not all authors, though, present mitigating factors that would help to establish motivation, however pathological. In the earliest ballad texts, underlying motivation for the demonic behavior of the returning lover is vague and unspecified; in later versions the demon-lover justifies his behavior by stating that it is revenge that drives him to destroy his victim, for she had married someone else. As a motive, revenge appears to be a relatively recent addition to the ballad and was added no doubt because without some kind of motivating factor, such inhumane cruelty is more disturbing than it would be with an explanation. In *Wuthering Heights, Tess of the d'Urbervilles,* "The Princess," and "The Demon Lover," the authors are careful to provide motivating factors which are more or less satisfactory explanations for the cruelty demon-lovers perpetrate on their victims. Although the authors do not condone victimization, they provide mitigating factors which help to make their stories more believable. *Dracula,* however, is terrifying expressly because Count Dracula destroys women randomly without any discernible motivation behind his cruelty whatsoever, aside from his need for blood.

Demon-lover figures, then, are associated with violence, evil, and the demonic. Very few contemporary psychologists or psychiatrists believe in demons or in demon possession or advocate theories that deal with complex questions of evil; or if they do, most do not admit to it, at least professionally. Rollo May provides his definition of the demonic in *Love and Will,* asserting both its creative and destructive potential:

> The daimonic is *any natural function which has the power to take over the whole person.* Sex and eros, anger and rage, and the craving for power are examples. . . .
> The daimonic is the urge in every being to affirm itself, assert itself, perpetuate and increase itself. The daimonic becomes evil when it usurps the total self without regard to the integration of that self, or to the unique forms and desires of others and their need for integration. It then appears as excessive aggression, hostility, cruelty—the things about ourselves which horrify us most, and which we repress whenever we can or, more likely, project on others. [P. 123]

Although May theorizes about demonic possession, he underplays the role of evil by defining "daimonic" as a natural drive to create and to assert oneself; the demonic runs amok and becomes destructive when a person who feels lonely and powerless strikes out. "To inflict pain and torture at least proves that one can affect somebody," May writes (p. 31). May, however, denies the influence of an outside force, stating that if the demonic is purely objective, that is, exists outside of the individual, there is a chance of "sliding into superstition in which man is simply the victim of external powers" (p. 136). On the other hand, according to May, if the demonic exists within the individual, "you take it purely subjectively, you psychologize the daimonic; everything tends to be a projection" (p. 136). As a way of reconciling this problem, he suggests, "If we think of the daimonic as man's struggle with forces from within his own unconscious which, at the same time, are rooted in the objective world, we can understand how this conflict would be brought closer to the surface, made more demanding and available" (p. 170).

In a recent exploration of evil, *People of the Lie: The Hope for Healing Human Evil*, M. Scott Peck deviates from his colleagues in the psychiatric community by proposing a clinical appreciation of evil, a recognition that some patients are supernaturally possessed by the power of evil and thereby commit heinous acts of physical or psychological violence against other people. Peck advocates treating evil as a mental disorder and outlines specific characteristics attributable to patients who suffer from this condition:

> The time is right, I believe, for psychiatry to recognize a distinct new type of personality disorder to encompass those I have named evil. In addition to the abrogation of responsibility that characterizes all personality disorders, this one would specifically be distinguished by:
>
> (a) consistent destructive, scapegoating behavior, which may often be quite subtle.
>
> (b) excessive, albeit usually covert, intolerance to criticism and other forms of narcissistic injury.
>
> (c) pronounced concern with a public image and self-image of respectability, contributing to a stability of life-style but also to pretentiousness and denial of hateful feelings or vengeful motives.
>
> (d) intellectual deviousness, with an increased like-

lihood of a mild schizophreniclike disturbance of thinking at times of stress. [P. 129]

Peck is referring, of course, to extreme cases of consistent and
excessive self-protective behavior which results in injury to
others. His work fills a gap in our understanding of deviant
behavior; it explains why certain individuals habitually deceive themselves and others and how their pathological cruelty allows them to destroy people who are caught unaware
in their diabolical trap.

Deception played a major part in the Devil's ability to snare
his victims, according to accounts by accused "witches" during the Middle Ages and the Renaissance (see chapter 2).
Deception also plays a major part in the demon-lover motif,
as the demon-lover figures in the ballad texts and in the literature discussed in this study all deceive their victims in one
way or another. What makes demon-lover tales terrifying yet
fascinating is the deceptive way in which victims are snared
by human representatives of evil. Lovelace, Heathcliff, and
Alec d'Urberville, to name only three leading demon-lover
figures, terrify and fascinate both their victims and the readers
of their stories. While literary critics have often been at a loss
fully to explain their appeal, Peck's description of what he
calls "people of the lie" provides a psychological paradigm
for understanding the basis for the aggressive behavior of
demon-lovers. Regarding the connection between pretense
and reality, Peck states, "The words 'image,' 'appearance,' and
'outwardly' are crucial to understanding the morality of the
evil, While they ["people of the lie"] seem to lack any motivation to *be* good, they intensely desire to appear good. Their
'goodness' is all on a level of pretense. It is, in effect, a lie.
This is why they are the 'people of the lie' " (p. 75). Peck's
observations regarding the duplicity of those connected with
evil describe the behavior of demon-lovers found in many
works of literature. For example, after having been away for
three years, Heathcliff returns to Wuthering Heights transformed into a gentleman, yet with revenge in his heart. Alec
d'Urberville attempts to seduce Tess by providing for her

family, yet the bad fortune to which her family is subjected causes the reader to suspect that Alec may have had a hand in arranging for their desperate search for shelter. In the ballad, the demon-lover pretends to be wealthy, a pretense he adopts to lure his victim onto his ship in order to take her to sea, where he drowns her.

Peck further describes evil people as having the following characteristics: the desire to confuse (p. 179); a strong need to control, along with a sense of panic and dread of losing control (p. 181); a lust for power (p. 177); loneliness (p. 190); and the refusal to acknowledge sin (p. 69).[27] Furthermore, Peck suggests that since evil people "must deny their own badness, they must perceive others as bad. They *project* their own evil onto the world" (p. 74); they must, he contends, project their own denied pain, caused by guilt, onto scapegoats (p. 123). Peck helps us to answer the question regarding the motivation behind the destructive behavior of demon-lovers when, thinking of "people of the lie," he writes: "What possesses them, drives them? Basically, it is fear. They are terrified that the pretense will break down and they will be exposed to the world and to themselves. They are continually frightened that they will come face-to-face with their own evil" (p. 124).

According to Peck, the inexplicable cruelty committed by people similar to the demon-lovers focused upon in this study may be explained by a combination of factors which open certain individuals to the influence of evil, specifically, loneliness, the inability to engage in self-reflection, and a lust for power. Given these conditions, Peck suggests, men (and women, too, of course) sometimes submit to the power of evil as a way of controlling their experience, and as a result they victimize others who cross their paths. It is fear, Peck asserts, that binds them to their diabolically destructive behavioral patterns. Basically, then, fictional demon-lovers are fundamentally insecure men who feel compelled to victimize women because of their own inability or unwillingness to confront themselves, to explore their own feelings of emptiness, to examine their own potential for evil. This inability to suffer emotional pain, Peck tells us, "usually lies at the very root of emotional illness" (p. 123); through projection and scapegoating, the pain is deflected from the one denying the pain, thereby permitting him to avoid the stark awareness of his own inadequacies and imperfections (p. 123).

Jung essentially affirms the same belief regarding the underlying purpose of projection when he writes, "Projections change the world into the replica of one's own unknown face" (*Aion*, p. 9). May raises the concept of projection out of the realm of the personal and comments on the geocentric tendency of nations to project evil onto other nations: "Thus our tendency to see in every communist a devil, to identify ourselves with God, and to fight no wars but only undertake crusades. . . . The enemy becomes the carrier of the elements we repress in ourselves. We fight our adversaries little realizing that we are fighting our own selves, denied though it be" (pp. 158-59). By projecting his "shadow," or the unacknowledged negative sides of his psyche, onto another, specifically a woman, a demon-lover is then able to victimize her as she is seen as a threat to his psychological well-being; in this way, the demon-lover figure is able to preserve his false sense of self and thereby avoid emotional pain. Projection allows the demon-lovers in the literature under discussion to control their worlds. Peck considers the fundamental problem of human evil as closely aligned to narcissism; his views bring to mind the characteristics of the demon-lovers encountered in many important works of nineteenth- and twentieth-century fiction:

> Theirs is a brand of narcissism so total that they [evil people] seem to lack, in whole or in part, this capacity for empathy. . . .
> We can see, then, that their narcissism makes the evil dangerous not only because it motivates them to scapegoat others but also because it deprives them of the restraint that results from empathy and respect for others. In addition to the fact that the evil need victims to sacrifice to their narcissism, their narcissism permits them

to ignore the humanity of their victims as well. As it gives them the motive for murder, so it also renders them insensitive to the act of killing. The blindness of the narcissist to others can extend even beyond a lack of empathy; narcissists may not 'see' others at all. [pp. 136-37]

The victimization that occurs at the hands of demon-lovers is vindictive, punitive, and hostile. In the ballad, justification for such victimization is lacking for the most part; in the same way, Heathcliff's behavior cannot be fully accounted for by examining his childhood experiences either before or after he arrived at the Earnshaw home. The deliberate victimization that occurs in the other works of literature discussed in this study is difficult to explain also except by attributing a quality of evil to the demon-lover figures.

For victimization to occur, there must be victims, women in this case, who assume the role due to their own sense of powerlessness. The victims of the ballad as well as the literature in some way permit themselves to be dominated by sadistic would-be lovers. Peck calls this social arrangement "thralldom," pointing out that the most common form of one person's having dominion over another is a parent-child relationship, as the child is basically powerless and inexperienced while the parent seems, at least to the child, powerful and omnipotent. It is logical to assume, then, that where these same conditions exist within adult relationships, the possibility for thralldom also exists. In folklore and in traditional literature, relationships in which a woman becomes "in thrall" to a man are extremely common, though not all fit the particular plot formula expressed in the ballad complex. Peck reminds us that the theme is a common one in folk literature: "The theme of thralldom is not infrequent in fairy tales and myths in which princes and princesses and other beings have become captive to the evil power of some wicked witch or demon" (p. 117). Victims, Peck contends, must accept some of the responsibility for their own victimization.

Catherine Earnshaw becomes so enthralled with Heathcliff

that she firmly believes her own words when she exclaims, "I *am* Heathcliff!" Their symbiotic relationship demonstrates the attempt to dissolve ego boundaries, to obliterate selfhood, that may occur with thralldom as Peck presents it, for the victim is finally consumed by the victimizer. In *Tess of the d'Urbervilles*, Tess, innocent and childlike, responds to Alec as a somewhat cautious child might to a stranger who demonstrates a little too much affection. As shown in chapter 4, Alec dominates Tess from the beginning of their relationship, while she relinquishes her will to him over and over again. Alec clearly seeks to possess Tess; by possessing her, he believes he gains mastery over her innocence and purity. Alec projects his own unacknowledged evil onto Tess and tries to dominate her, thereby attempting to conquer his own ego-threatening "shadow," to apply Jung's term. Heathcliff and Alec are incapable of confronting their own potential for evil, and to safeguard their carefully constructed views of reality, they victimize women who are vulnerable and impressionable and who exhibit a tendency to deny what is actually happening. *Wuthering Heights* is the exception as Catherine participates in the mutual victimization that develops between Heathcliff and her. On the other hand, in Lawrence's "The Princess," Dollie refuses to remain cognizant of the danger she is in as she follows Romero up the mountain path which leads to her destruction. In the same way, in Elizabeth Bowen's "The Demon Lover," Kathleen Drover fails to rely on her intuition regarding the danger she is in when she returns to her old home in London. If she had paid attention to the terror she felt and if she had relied upon her memories and associations about her former soldier-lover—his cruelty and his unnatural obsession with her—she could have saved herself. In other words, she could have chosen *not* to be a victim. Like the women in the demon-lover tales told by fiction writers over the last two hundred years, the woman in the ballad perhaps *could* have prevented her tragedy had she trusted herself more, had she been more alert to the danger she was in, and had she relied on her own sense of self-preservation. Why a woman would allow herself to be victimized is dif-

ficult to explain. Two contemporary writers have contributed
important insights about this problem, Stanton Peele, who
introduced the concept of addiction to relationships in *Love
and Addiction*, and Robin Norwood, who describes in detail
in *Women Who Love Too Much* the process of forming dam-
aging, addictive relationships and provides the steps necessary to put a stop to one's victimization.

Peele's work introduces the revolutionary idea that people
may become attracted to one another explicitly because their
insecurities, their fears, and their needs mesh, and thus their
being together meets an unconscious desire to remain psychologically unhealthy. According to Peele, addiction to relationships is formed in the same manner and basically for
the same reasons as addiction to alcohol or drugs: dependency
results when one has a deep and significant need to avoid
oneself.

Relying on Peele's work for her theoretical backdrop, Norwood focuses on women who become obsessed with men to
the point of victimizing themselves, women who, like the
woman in the ballad, abandon their lives and themselves.
Norwood attributes this self-victimizing behavior to low self-
esteem and fear of confronting oneself. In her clinical practice,
Norwood observed many women who, as a result of being
raised in dysfunctional or chaotic homes, quite literally developed addictions to men. These women, Norwood believes,
tend to repeat early childhood experiences in order to master
them once and for all. Women whose fathers were "emotionally unavailable," for instance, tend to choose emotionally
unavailable men because that is what they are used to and
because they believe that finally they will "win" the love that
was kept from them during childhood. D.H. Lawrence demonstrates this exact causal relationship in "The Princess" as
Dollie's mother and father prove to be dysfunctional, leaving
Dollie emotionally crippled and unable to function well in
society. When she meets Romero, her demon-lover, she instantly attaches herself to him and begins to deny the reality
of her threatening situation. Thus, when she is subsequently
faced with a dangerous situation, she obliterates her con-

sciousness and adjusts reality to better fit her fabricated version of her experience; as a result, Dollie allows herself to be victimized, to be violated by a man who is compared to her father several times in the course of the narrative. According to Peele and Norwood, women cannot be victimized unless they allow themselves to be, and the ballad as well as the literature bear this out. Out of their own insecurities they place themselves in positions where they are likely to become victimized. Catherine Earnshaw, Tess Durbeyfield, and Dollie Urquhart clearly come from the kinds of dysfunctional families that Norwood identifies as creating women who tend to become victims. And when pathologically cruel men interact with women primed for victimization, the demon-lover arrangement is initiated.[28]

Throughout the centuries, ballad singers and fiction writers have reflected the dynamics represented by this motif for two fundamental reasons. First, people feel compelled to remind themselves over and over again about the danger of joining forces with the power of evil. Second, demon-lover tales have functioned as a subtle means of controlling women by repeating both in folk culture and in popular culture the causal relationship between ignoring the accepted norms of society and destruction. Samuel Richardson wrote *Clarissa* and Thomas Hardy wrote *Tess* as warnings to women to avoid heartless, insensitive rakes,[29] just as the earliest known version of "The Demon Lover" ballad began as a "Warning to Married Women," who were urged to be faithful to their husbands lest evil destroy them.

Demon-lover tales will no doubt always be with us, especially in times of societal stress and rapid change when people feel powerless and out of control. We respond to these stories out of our own fears and anxieties and we are drawn to them because of our urge to reconcile our destructive "shadow" selves with another side of ourselves—the vulnerable victim. Demon-lover stories provide safe, objective ways to examine the dynamics of our own interior worlds; furthermore, they provide creative foci for unconscious projections. "The Demon Lover" and the literature patterned after the ballad reflect the same basic conflict projected by generations of balladeers, authors, listeners, and readers, a conflict between aggression and victimization and between power and powerlessness.

# APPENDIX A

# Child Ballad Texts

[From Francis James Child, ed., *The English and Scottish Popular Ballads*, pp. 362-69.]

A

Pepys Ballads, IV, 101; from a copy in Percy's papers.

1 There dwelt a fair maid in the West,
   Of worthy birth and fame,
  Neer unto Plimouth, stately town,
   Jane Reynolds was her name.

2 This damsel dearly was belovd
   By many a proper youth,
  And what of her is to be said
   Is known for very truth.

3 Among the rest a seaman brave
   Unto her a wooing came;
  A comely proper youth he was,
   James Harris calld by name.

4 The maid and young man was agreed,
   As time did them allow,
  And to each other secretly
   They made a solemn vow,

5 That they would ever faithfull be
   Whilst Heaven afforded life;
  He was to be her husband kind,
   And she his faithfull wife.

6 A day appointed was also
   When they was to be married;
  But before these things were brought to pass
   Matters were strangely carried.

7 All you that faithfull lovers be
  Give ear and hearken well,
  And what of them became at last
  I will directly tell.

8 The young man he was prest to sea,
  and forcëd was to go;
  His sweet-heart she must stay behind,
  Whether she would or no.

9 And after he was from her gone
  She three years for him staid,
  Expecting of his comeing home,
  And kept herself a maid.

10 At last news came that he was dead
   Within a forraign land,
   And how that he was buried
   She well did understand,

11 For whose sweet sake the maiden she
   Lamented many a day,
   And never was she known at all
   The wanton for to play.

12 A carpenter that livd hard by,
   When he heard of the same,
   Like as the other had done before,
   To her a wooing came.

13 But when that he had gained her love
   They married were with speed,
   And four years space, being man and wife,
   They loveingly agreed.

14 Throo pritty childien in this time
   This loving couple had,
   Which made their father's heart rejoyce,
   And mother wondrous glad.

15 But as occasion servd, one time
   The good man took his way
   Some three days journey from his home,
   Intending not to stay.

16 But, whilst that he was gone away,
   A spirit in the night

Came to the window of his wife,
  And did her sorely fright.

17 Which spirit spake like to a man,
     And unto her did say,
   'My dear and onely love,' quoth he,
     'Prepare and come away.

18 'James Harris is my name,' quoth he,
     'Whom thou didst love so dear,
   And I have traveld for thy sake
     At least this seven year.

19 'And now I am returnd again,
     To take thee to my wife,
   And thou with me shalt go to sea,
     To end all further strife.'

20 'O tempt me not, sweet James,' quoth she,
     'With thee away to go;
   If I should leave my children small,
     Alas! what would they do?

21 'My husband is a carpenter,
     A carpenter of great fame;
   I would not for five hundred pounds
     That he should know the same.'

22 'I might have had a king's daughter,
     And she would have married me;
   But I forsook her golden crown,
     And for the love of thee.

23 'Therefore, if thou'lt thy husband forsake,
     And thy children three also,
   I will forgive the[e] what is past,
     If thou wilt with me go.'

24 'If I forsake my husband and
     My little children three,
   What means hast thou to bring me to,
     If I should go with thee?'

25 'I have seven ships upon the sea;
     When they are come to land,
   Both marriners and marchandize
     Shall be at thy command.

26 'The ship wherein my love shall sail
   Is glorious to behold;
   The sails shall be of finest silk,
   And the mast of shining gold.'

27 When he had told her these fair tales,
   To love him she began,
   Because he was in human shape,
   Much like unto a man.

28 And so together away they went
   From off the English shore,
   And since that time the woman-kind
   Was never seen no more.

29 But when her husband he come home
   And found his wife was gone,
   And left her three sweet pretty babes
   Within the house alone,

30 He beat his breast, he tore his hair,
   The tears fell from his eyes,
   And in the open streets he run
   With heavy doleful cries.

31 And in this sad distracted case
   He hangd himself for woe
   Upon a tree near to the place;
   The truth of all is so.

32 The children now are fatherless,
   And left without a guide,
   But yet no doubt the heavenly powers
   Will for them well provide.


B

The Rambler's Garland, British Museum, 11621, c. 4 (57).
1785(?)

1 'Well met, well met, my own true love,
   Long time I have been seeking thee;
   I am lately come from the salt sea,
   And all for the sake, love, of thee.

2 'I might have had a king's daughter,
   And fain she would have married me;
   But I've forsaken all her crowns of gold,
   And all for the sake, love, of thee.'

3 'If you might have had a king's daughter,
   I think you much to blame;
   I would not for five hundred pounds
   That my husband should hear the same.

4 'For my husband is a carpenter,
   And a young ship-carpenter is he,
   And by him I have a little son.
   Or else, love, I'd go along with thee.

5 'But if I should leave my husband dear,
   Likewise my little son also,
   What have you to maintain me withal,
   If I along with you should go?'

6 'I have seven ships upon the seas,
   And one of them brought me to land,
   And seventeen mariners to wait on thee,
   For to be, love, at your command.

7 'A pair of slippers thou shalt have,
   They shall be made of beaten gold,
   Nay and be lin'd with velvet soft,
   For to keep thy feet from cold.

8 'A gilded boat thou then shall have,
   The oars shall gilded be also,
   And mariners to row the[e] along,
   For to keep thee from thy overthrow.'

9 They had not been long upon the sea
   Before that she began to weep:
   'What, weep you for my gold?' he said,
   'Or do you weep for my fee?

10 'Or do you weep for some other young man
   That you love much better than me?'
   'No, I do weep for my little son,
   That should have come along with me.'

11 She had not been upon the seas
    Passing days three or four

But the mariner and she were drowned,
And never were heard of more.

12 When tidings to old England came
The ship-carpenter's wife was drownd.
He wrung his hands and tore his hair,
And grievously fell in a swoon.

13 'Oh cursed be those mariners!
For they do lead a wicked life;
They ruind me, a ship-carpenter,
By deluding away my wife.'


C
Buchan's Ballads of the North of Scotland, I, 214.

1 'O are ye my father? Or are ye my mother?
Or are ye my brother John?
Or are ye James Herries, my first true-love,
Come back to Scotland again?'

2 'I am not your father, I am not your mother,
Nor am I your brother John;
But I'm James Herries, your first true-love,
Come back to Scotland again.'

3 'Awa, awa, ye former lovers,
Had far awa frae me!
For now I am another man's wife
Ye'll neer see joy o me.'

4 'Had I kont that ere I came here,
I neer had come to thee;
For I might hae married the king's daughter,
Sae fain she woud had me.

5 'I despised the crown o gold,
The yellow silk also,
And I am come to my true-love,
But with me she'll not go.'

6 'My husband he is a carpenter,
Makes his bread on dry land,

And I hae born him a young son;
Wi you I will not gang.'

7 'You must forsake your dear husband,
Your little young son also,
Wi me to sail the raging seas,
Where the stormy winds do blow.'

8 'O what hae you to keep me wi,
If I should with you go,
If I'd forsake my dear husband,
My little young son also?'

9 'See ye not yon seven pretty ships?
The eighth brought me to land,
With merchandize and mariners,
And wealth in every hand.'

10 She turnd her round upon the shore
Her love's ships to behold;
Their topmasts and their mainyards
Were coverd oer wi gold.

11 Then she's gane to her little young son,
And kissd him cheek and chin;
Sae has she to her sleeping husband,
And dune the same to him.

12 'O sleep ye, wake ye, my husband?
I wish ye wake in time!
I woudna for ten thousand pounds
This night ye knew my mind.'

13 She's drawn the slippers on her feet,
Were coverd oer wi gold,
Well lined within wi velvet fine,
To had her frae the cold.

14 She hadna sailed upon the sea
A league but barely three
Till she minded on her dear husband,
Her little young son tee.

15 'O gin I were at land again,
At land where I woud be,
The woman neer shoud bear the son
Shoud gar me sail the sea.'

16 'O hold your tongue, my sprightly flower,
   Let a' your mourning be;
   I'll show you how the lilies grow
   On the banks o Italy.'

17 She hadna sailed on the sea
   A day but barely ane
   Till the thoughts o grief came in her mind,
   And she langd for to be hame.

18 'O gentle death, come cut my breath,
   I may be dead ere morn!
   I may be buried in Scottish ground,
   Where I was bred and born!'

19 'O hold your tongue, my lily leesome thing,
   Let a' your mourning be;
   But for a while we'll stay at Rose Isle,
   Then see a far countrie.

20 'Ye'se neer be buried in Scottish ground,
   Nor land ye's nae mair see;
   I brought you away to punish you
   For the breaking your vows to me.

21 'I said ye shoud see the lilies grow
   On the banks o Italy;
   But I'll let you see the fishes swim,
   In the bottom o the sea.'

22 He reached his hand to the topmast,
   Made a' the sails gae down,
   And in the twinkling o an ee
   Baith ship and crew did drown.

23 The fatal flight o this wretched maid
   Did reach her ain countrie;
   Her husband then distracted ran,
   And this lament made he:

24 'O wae be to the ship, the ship,
   And wae be to the sea,
   And wae be to the mariners
   Took Jeanie Douglas frae me!

25 'O bonny, bonny was my love,
   A pleasure to behold;

The very hair o my love's head
Was like the threads o gold.

26 'O bonny was her cheek, her cheek,
And bonny was her chin,
And bonny was the bride she was,
The day she was made mine!'

D

Kinloch MSS, I, 297; from the recitation of T. Kinnear,
Stonehaven.

1 'O whare hae ye been, my dearest dear,
These seven lang years and more?'
'O I am come to seek my former vows,
That ye promisd me before.'

2 'Awa wi your former vows,' she says,
'Or'else ye will breed strife;
Awa wi your former vows,' she says,
'For I'm become a wife.

3 'I am married to a ship-carpenter,
A ship-carpenter he's bound;
I wadna he kend my mind this nicht
For twice five hundred pound.'

. . . . . . . . . . . . . . . . . . . . . . . . . . .

4 She has put her foot on gude ship-board,
And on ship-board she's gane.
And the veil that hung oure her face
Was a' wi gowd begane.

5 She had na sailed a league, a league,
A league but barely twa,
Till she did mind on the husband she left,
And her wee young son alsua.

6 'O haud your tongue, my dearest dear,
Let all your follies abee;
I'll show whare the white lillies grow,
On the banks of Italie.'

7 She had na sailed a league, a league,
   A league but barely three,
   Till grim, grim grew his countenance,
   And gurly grew the sea.

8 'O haud your tongue, my dearest dear,
   Let all your follies abee;
   I'll show whare the white lillies grow,
   In the bottom of the sea.'

9 He's tane her by the milk-white hand,
   And he's thrown her in the main;
   And full five-and-twenty hundred ships
   Perishd all on the coast of Spain.


E
Motherwell's MS., p. 97.

1 Where have you been, my long lost lover,
   This seven long years and more?'
   'I've been seeking gold for thee, my love,
   And riches of great store.

2 'Now I'm come for the vows you promised me,
   You promised me long ago;'
   'My former vows you must forgive,
   For I'm a wedded wife.'

3 'I might have been married to a king's daughter,
   Far, far ayont the sea;
   But I refused the crown of gold,
   And it's all for the love of thee.'

4 'If you might have married a king's daughter,
   Yourself you have to blame;
   For I'm married to a ship's-carpenter,
   And to him I have a son.

5 'Have you any place to put me in,
   If I with you should gang?'
   'I've seven brave ships upon the sea,
   All laden to the brim.

6 'I'll build my love a bridge of steel,
  All for to help her oer;
  Likewise webs of silk down by her side,
  To keep my love from the cold.'

7 She took her eldest son into her arms,
  And sweetly did him kiss:
  'My blessing go with you, and your father too,
  For little does he know of this.'

8 As they were walking up the street,
  Most beautiful for to behold,
  He cast a glamour oer her face,
  And it shone like the brightest gold.

9 As they were walking along the sea-side,
  Where his gallant ship lay in,
  So ready was the chair of gold
  To welcome this lady in.

10 They had not sailed a league, a league,
  A league but scarsely three,
  Till altered grew his countenance,
  And raging grew the sea.

11 When they came to yon sea-side,
  She set her down to rest;
  It's then she spied his cloven foot,
  Most bitterly she wept.

12 'O is it for gold that you do weep?
  Or is it for fear?
  Or is it for the man you left behind
  When that you did come here?'

13 'It is not for gold that I do weep,
  O no, nor yet for fear;
  But it is for the man I left behind
  When that I did come here.

14 'O what a bright, bright hill is yon,
  That shines so clear to see?'
  'O it is the hill of heaven,' he said,
  'Where you shall never be.'

15 'O what a black, dark hill is yon,
  That looks so dark to me?'

'O it is the hill of hell,' he said,
    'Where you and I shall be.

16 'Would you wish to see the fishes swim
    In the bottom of the sea,
  Or wish to see the leaves grow green
    On the banks of Italy?'

17 'I hope I'll never see the fishes swim
    On the bottom of the sea,
  But I hope to see the leaves grow green
    On the banks of Italy.'

18 He took her up to the topmast high,
    To see what she could see;
  He sunk the ship in a flash of fire,
    To the bottom of the sea.

F

Minstrelsy of the Scottish Border, fifth edition, 1812, II,
427; taken down from the recitation of Walter Grieve by
William Laidlaw.

1 'O where have you been, my long, long love,
    This long seven years and mair?'
  'O I'm come to seek my former vows
    Ye granted me before.'

2 'O hold your tongue of your former vows,
    For they will breed sad strife;
  O hold your tongue of your former vows,
    For I am become a wife.'

3 He turned him right and round about,
    And the tear blinded his ee:
  'I wad never hae trodden on Irish ground,
    If it had not been for thee.

4 'I might hae had a king's daughter,
    Far, far beyond the sea;
  I might have had a king's daughter,
    Had it not been for love o thee.'

5 'If ye might have had a king's daughter,
   Yer sel ye had to blame;
Ye might have taken the king's daughter,
   For ye kend that I was nane.

6 'If I was to leave my husband dear,
   And my two babes also,
O what have you to take me to,
   If with you I should go?'

7 'I hae seven ships upon the sea—
   The eighth brought me to land—
With four-and-twenty bold mariners,
   And music on every hand.'

8 She has taken up her two little babes,
   Kissd them baith cheek and chin:
'O fair ye weel, my ain two babes,
   For I'll never see you again.'

9 She set her foot upon the ship,
   No mariners could she behold;
But the sails were o the taffetie,
   And the masts o the beaten gold.

10 She had not sailed a league, a league,
   A league but barely three,
When dismal grew his countenance,
   And drumlie grew his ee.

11 They had not saild a league, a league,
   A league but barely three,
Until she espied his cloven foot,
   And she wept right bitterlie.

12 'O hold your tongue of your weeping,' says he.
   'Of your weeping now let me be;
I will shew you how the lilies grow
   On the banks of Italy.'

13 'O what hills are yon, yon pleasant hills,
   That the sun shines sweetly on?'
'O yon are the hills of heaven,' he said,
   'Where you will never win.'

14 'O whaten a mountain is yon,' she said,
   'All so dreary wi frost and snow?'

'O yon is the mountain of hell,' he cried,
  Where you and I will go.'

15 He strack the tap-mast wi his hand,
  The fore-mast wi his knee,
And he brake that gallant ship in twain,
  And sank her in the sea.


G
Motherwell's Minstrelsy, p. 93.

1 'I have seven ships upon the sea,
  Laden with the finest gold,
And mariners to wait us upon;
  All these you may behold.

2 'And I have shoes for my love's feet,
  Beaten of the purest gold,
And linëd wi the velvet soft,
  To keep my love's feet from the cold.

3 'O how do you love the ship?' he said,
  'Or how do you love the sea?
And how do you love the bold mariners
  That wait upon thee and me?'

4 'O I do love the ship,' she said.
  'And I do love the sea;
But woe be to the dim mariners,
  That nowhere I can see!'

5 They had not sailed a mile awa,
  Never a mile but one,
When she began to weep and mourn,
  And to think on her little wee son.

6 'O hold your tongue, my dear,' he said,
  'And let all your weeping abee,
For I'll soon show to you how the lilies grow
  On the banks of Italy.'

7 They had not sailed a mile awa,
  Never a mile but two,

Until she espied his cloven foot.
From his gay robes sticking thro.

8 They had not sailed a mile awa,
  Never a mile but three.
When dark, dark, grew his eerie looks,
  And raging grew the sea.

9 They had not sailed a mile awa,
  Never a mile but four,
when the little wee ship ran round about.
  And never was seen more.


### H

Christie, Traditional Ballad Airs, I, 138; taken down by
the editor's father from the singing of an aged relative.

1 He's given her a pair of shoes,
  To hold her frae the cold;
The one side of them was velvaret,
  And the other beaten gold.

2 Up she has taen her little wee son,
  And given him kisses three;
Says, Fare ye weel, my little wee son,
  I'm gaun to sail the sea.

# APPENDIX B

## Davis Ballad Texts

[From Arthur Kyle Davis, Jr.,
*Traditional Ballads of Virginia* (Charlottesville:
University Press of Virginia, 1929, 1969), pp. 440-50.
Reprinted by permission of the publisher.]

### A

"The House Carpenter." Collected by Mr. Ben C.
Moomaw, Jr. Sung by Mr. Sam Pritt, of Barber, Va. Alleghany County. November 28, 1924.

1 "Well met, well met, my own true love,
  Well met, well met," said he,
"I've just returned from the salt, salt sea,
  And it's all for the sake of thee.

2 "Oh, I could have married the King's daughter, dear,
  And she would have married me,
But I have refused the crowns of gold,
  And it's all for the sake of thee."

3 "If you could have married the King's daughter, dear,
  I'm sure you are to blame;
For I am married to the house carpenter,
  And he is a fine young man."

4 "If you'll forsake your house carpenter
  And go along with me,
I'll take you to where the grass grows green
  On the banks of the Sweet Willie.

5 "If I forsake my house carpenter
  And go along with thee,
What have you got to maintain me upon
  And keep me from slavery?"

6 "I've six ships sailing on the salt, salt sea,
  Sailing for dry land,
And a hundred and twenty jolly young men
  Shall be at your command."

7 Oh, she picked up her poor little babe
  And kisses gave it three,
  Saying, "Stay here with my house carpenter
  And keep him companie."

8 She dressed herself in rich attire,
  Most glorious to behold,
  And as she tread upon her road
  She shone like the glittering gold.

9 They had not sailed two weeks on sea,
  I'm sure it was not three,
  Till this fair maid began to weep,
  And she wept most bitterly.

10 "Oh, do you weep for my gold?" he said,
   "My houses, my land, or my store?
   Or do you weep for your house carpenter
   That you never shall see any more?"

11 "I do not weep for your gold," she said,
   "Your houses, your land, nor your store;
   But I do weep for my poor little babe
   That I never shall see any more."

12 "Oh, what is that that shines so white,
   That shines as white as snow?"
   "Oh, those are the hills of Heaven itself,
   Where we may never go."

13 "Oh, what is that that shines so black,
   That shines as black as a crow?"
   "Oh, that is the clouds of Hell itself,
   Where you and I must go."

14 They had not sailed three weeks on sea,
   I'm sure it was not four,
   Till in the ship there sprung a leak,
   And she sank to rise no more.

15 "Oh, cursed be a sailor's life
   And an o'er-persuading man
   That stole me from my house carpenter
   And took away my life."

B
"The House Carpenter." Collected by Mr. John Stone.
Sung by Mr. George Hart, of Konnarock, Va. Washington
County. November 8, 1921.

1 "Well met, well met, my old true love,
Well met, well met," says he.
"I'm just returning from the sea, salt sea,
All for the sake of thee.

2 "I once could have married a king's daughter dear,
And she would have married me;
But I have refused her crowns of gold,
And it's all for the sake of thee."

3 "If you could have married a king's daughter dear,
I'm sure you are to blame;
For I am married to a house carpenter,
And I believe he is a fine young man."

4 "If you will forsake your house carpenter
And go along with me,
I'll take you to where the grass grows green
On the banks of the Sweet Willoree."

5 "If I was to forsake my house carpenter
And go along with thee,
What would you have to maintain me on
Or to keep me from slavery?"

6 "I have three ships all sailing on sea,
All sailing for dry land,
One hundred and ten brave bold young men;
You can have them at your command."

7 She picked up her sweet little babe
And kisses gave it three,
Saying, " You stay here, my sweet little babe,
And keep your pap company."

8 She went and she dressed in her richery,
She went along her way,
She shined and she glittered and she boldly walked
The streets of Purity.

9 They had n't been on board but about two weeks,
And I am sure not three,

Till this young lady began for to weep,
And she wept most bitterly.

10 She cursed all the female kind,
She cursed the sailor's life.
"You've robbed me of my house carpenter
And deprived me of my life."

11 "Is it for my gold that you weep?
Or is it for my store?
Or is it for your house carpenter
Whose face you'll see no more?"

12 "It's neither for your gold I weep,
Nor neither is it for your store;
It's for that sweet little babe of mine
Whose face I'll see no more."

13 They had n't been on board but about three weeks,
And I am sure not four,
Till this young lady began for to weep,
And her weeping ceased no more.

14 They had n't been on board but about four weeks,
And I am sure not five,
Till the vessel sprung a leak and it sunk
And it sunk for to never rise.


C

"The House Carpenter." Collected by Miss Alfreda M.
Peel. Sung by Miss Rushia Richardson, of Vinton, Va.,
and by Sis Sears, of Salem, Va. Roanoke County. September 11, 1922. With music.

1 "Well met, well met, my own fair lady,
Well met, well met," cried she,
"I've just returned from my castle,
All for the sake of thee."

2 "Too late, too late, my own fair knight,
Too late, too late," cried she,
"I've just been wed to a house carpenter,
And I think he's a nice young man."

3 "If you will leave your house carpenter
And come along with me,

I'll take you where the grass grows green
On the banks of the salt, salt sea.

4 "If you will leave your house-carpenter
And come along with me,
I'll take you where the grass grows green
Beside my castles three.

5 "I have three ships on the salt, salt sea,
They are sailing for my lands;
One hundred and ten so jolly knights
You can have at your command."

6 She picked up her sweet little babe,
And kisses gave it three,
Crying, "Stay at home, my little babe,
And keep him company."

7 She was not on the sea three weeks,
I'm sure it was not three,
Before this lady began to weep
And wept most bitterly.

8 "Oh, is it for my gold you weep?
Or is it for my store?"
"I'm weeping for my sweet little babe
That I shall see no more.

9 "If I live till another fall
And God will give me grace,
I'll buy a bottle of Jenico wine
To wash your deceitful face.

10 "I wish to the Lord I had never been born
And died when I was young;
I never would wet my rosy cheeks
With no man's lying tongue."

11 She was not on the sea three weeks,
I'm sure it was not four,
Before the ship began to sink,
And sank to rise no more.

D
" The House Carpenter." Collected by Miss Juliet Fauntleroy. Sung by Mrs. Jesse Maxie, of Altavista, Va. Camp-

bell County. February 19, 1914 and August 1, 1914. With music.

1 "I've come, I've come, my own true love,
   I've come, I've come," said he.
   "I've crossed the salty waters deep, ⎤
   And it's all for the love of thee. ⎦ *Repeat*

2 "I could have married a king's daughter fair,
   She would have married me,
   But 't was all for refuses of her silver and her gold,
   And all for the love of thee."

3 "If you could have married a king's daughter fair,
   I'm sure you are to blame;
   For I have married a house carpenter,
   I'm sure he's a nice young man."

4 "If you will leave your house carpenter
   And go along with me,
   I'll carry you where the grass grows green,
   On the banks of sweet Italy."

5 "If I should leave my house carpenter
   And go along with thee,
   What have you there to maintain me upon
   And keep me from a slav'ry?"

6 "I have a hundred ships on sail,
   All sailing for dry land,
   Five hundred and ten brave, jolly sailor men
   Shall be at your command."

7 She called to her side her sweet little babe,
   Her kisses was one, two, three,
   Saying, " Stay at home, my sweet little babe,
   And keep your papa company."

8 She had n't been on water two weeks,
   I'm sure it was not three,
   'Fore this fair lady she began to weep,
   And she wept most bitterly.

9 "Are you weeping for your money, my love?
   Are you weeping for your store?
   Are you weeping for your house carpenter
   That you left so far on shore?"

10 "No, I'm not weeping for my money, my love,
   Nor neither for my store;
   I'm weeping for my sweet little babe
   That I never shall see any more."

11 She had n't been on water three weeks,
   I'm sure it was not four,
   'Fore this fair lady she began to weep,
   And sank for to rise no more.

12 Come all of you now, nice young girls,
   Take warning now from me
   And never leave your house carpenter
   To go with a man on sea.


E
"On the Banks of the Sweet Laurie." Collected by Mr.
Wilson E. Somers, of Disputanta, Va. Found in Accomac
County. March 30, 1918.

1 "Well met, well met, my own true love,
   Well met, well met," cried he.
   "I have just returned from the sea, salt sea,
   And 't was all for the sake of thee;
   I have just returned from the sea, salt sea,
   And 't was all for the sake of thee.

2 "I could have married a king's daughter,
   So freely she'd marry me,
   But I refused her golden fee,
   And 'twas all for the sake of thee."

3 "If you could have married a king's daughter,
   I think you are to blame;
   For now I am married to a house carpenter,
   And I think him a fine young man."

4 "If you forsake your house carpenter
   And go along with me,
   I will take you where the grass grows green,
   On the banks of the Sweet Laurie."

5 "If I'll forsake my house carpenter
   And go along with thee,

What have you there to maintain a wife upon,
And keep her from slavery?"

6 "Six ships, six ships are now at sea,
Seven more are on dry land,
One hundred and ten all bold sailor men,
Shall be at your command."

7 She took her pretty and her sweet little babe,
And gave it kisses three,
Saving, "Stay at home with your own papa,
And he will be kind to thee."

8 She dressed herself in the finest silk,
And her waitress all in green,
And every city that they came to pass,
They took her to be some queen.

9 They had not sailed four weeks, four weeks,
Four weeks nor scarcely three,
When this lady fair, she began to weep,
And she wept most bitterly.

10 "Oh, why do you weep, my own true love?
Oh, why do you weep?" cried he.
"Oh, is it for your house or your house carpenter?
Or is it for your golden fee?"

11 "It's not for my house nor my house carpenter,
It's not for my golden fee,
But it is for my pretty and my sweet little babe
That I nevermore shall see."

12 They had not sailed five weeks, five weeks,
Five weeks nor scarcely four,
When this gallant ship, she began to sink,
And she sank to rise no more.

13 Oh, cursèd be these fair-faced men,
And cursèd be their lives;
They are always robbing house carpenters
And carrying away their wives.

F
" The House Carpenter." Collected by Mr. John Stone.
Sung by Miss Lottie Shaffir, of Mustoe, Va., who got it

from her mother, Mrs. L. A. Shaffir. Highland County.
November 3, 1920.

1  "We've met, we've met," cried he,
    "I've just returned from the salt, salt sea,
   And it was all for the sake of thee,
   And it was all for the sake of thee."

2  "I could have married the king's daughter fair
    And I know she would of (have?) married me,
   But I refused all crowns of gold
    And 't was for the sake of thee."

3  "If you could of married the king's daughter fair,
    I am sure you are for the blame;
   For I am married to a house carpenter
    And he is a fine young man."

4  "If you will forsake your house carpenter
    And go along with me,
   I'll take you to where the grass grows green
    On the banks of Sweet Valley."

5  "If I forsake my house carpenter
    And go along with you,
   What have you to maintain me upon
    And keep me from slavery?"

6  "I have seven ships all on the sea
    Sailing for dry land,
   A hundred and ten bold jolly young men,
    And they shall be at your command."

7  She picked up her pretty little babe
    And kisses gave it three,
   Saying, "Stay at home, my pretty little babe,
    And keep your father company."

8  She dressed herself in richrey,
    Most beauty to behold;
   And as she walked along the way
    She showed like glittering gold.

9  She had not been on sea two weeks,
    I am sure it was not three,
   Until fair Ellen began for to weep,
    And she wept most bitterly.

10 "It's what do you weep for? My gold?" he said,
    "Or do you weep for my store?
  Or do you weep for that house carpenter
    That you never shall see any more?"

11 "I do not weep for your gold," she said,
    "Nor do I weep for your store;
  But I do weep for my pretty little babe
    That I never shall see any more."

12 She had not been on sea three weeks,
    I am sure it was not four,
  Until her ship it sprang a leak,
    And she sank to rise no more.

13 "It's woe be unto a wayfaring man,
    And curses to a sailor,
  For robbing me of my house carpenter
    And taking away my life."


                    G

"The House Carpenter." Collected by Miss Martha M.
Davis, of Harrisonburg, Va. Fairfax County. August 14,
1914. With music. From the recitation of an old woman
who goes out to nurse. She learned it from other children
forty or fifty years ago when she was a child in Fairfax
County, Va." (Miss Davis).

1 "Well met, well met, my own true love,
    Well met, well met," says he;
  "I've just returned from the salt, salt sea,
    And it's all for love of thee.

2 "I could have married the king's daughter fair."
    "You might as well," said she,
  "For now I'm married to a house carpenter,
    And a nice young man is he."

3 "If you will forsake your house carpenter
    And go along with me,
  I'll carry you away where the grass grows green
    On the isle of sweet Willee."

4 "If I forsake my house carpenter
   And go away with thee,
   What have you to maintain me on
   Or keep me from slavery?"

5 "I have ten ships on the sea sailing wide,
   A-making on for land;
   One hundred of my bold sailor men
   Will be at your command."

6 She took her babe up in her arms
   And kisses gave it three.
   "Now stay at home, my sweet little babe,
   For your father's company."

7 She dressed herself in her richest to wear,
   And the weather being cold,
   She walked, she walked the streets around,
   She glittered like beaten gold.

8 She had n't been sailing more than two weeks,
   I'm sure it was not three,
   Before this damsel began for to weep,
   And she wept most bitterly.

9 "What are you weeping for, silver or gold?
   Are you weeping for my store?
   Are you weeping for your house carpenter
   You never shall see any more?"

10 "I neither weep for your silver nor gold,
   Nor do I weep for your store;
   I'm weeping for my sweet little babe
   I never shall see any more."

11 She had n't been sailing more than three weeks,
   I'm sure it was not four,
   Before this ship had sprung a leak
   And sunk to rise no more.

12 A curse, a curse to this young man
   That sails the ocean wide;
   He has robbed the poor house carpenter
   And taken away his bride.

# APPENDIX C

# Miscellaneous Ballad Texts

THE DÆMON-LOVER
[From Sir Walter Scott, *Minstrelsy of the Scottish Border*,
T.F. Henderson, ed., pp. 248-52.]

1 'O where have you been, my long, long love,
   This long seven years and more?'
   'O I'm come to seek my former vows,
   Ye granted me before.'

2 'O hold your tongue of your former vows,
   For they will breed sad strife;
   O hold your tongue of your former vows,
   For I am become a wife.'

3 He turn'd him right and round about,
   And the tear blinded his ee;
   'I wad never hae trodden on Irish ground,
   If it had not been for thee.

4 'I might have had a king's daughter,
   Far, far beyond the sea;
   I might have had a king's daughter,
   Had it not been for love o' thee.'

5 'If ye might have had a king's daughter,
   Yersell ye had to blame;
   Ye might have taken the king's daughter,
   For ye kend that I was nane.'

6 'O faulse are the vows of womankind,
   But fair is their faulse bodie;
   I never wad hae trodden on Irish ground,
   Had it not been for love o' thee.'

7 'If I was to leave my husband dear,
   And my two babes also,
   O what have you to take me to,
   If with you I should go?'

8 'I hae seven ships upon the sea,
   The eighth brought me to land;
   With four-and-twenty bold mariners,
   And music on every hand.'

9 She has taken up her two little babes,
   Kiss'd them baith cheek and chin;
   'O fair ye weel, my ain two babes,
   For I'll never see you again.'

10 She set her foot upon the ship,
   No mariners could she behold;
   But the sails were o' the taffetie,
   And the masts o' the beaten gold.

11 She had not sail'd a league, a league,
   A league but barely three,
   When dismal grew his countenance,
   And drumlie grew his ee.

12 The masts, that were like the beaten gold,
   Bent not on the heaving seas;
   But the sails, that were o' the taffetie,
   Fill'd not in the east land breeze.

13 They had not sail'd a league, a league,
   A league but barely three,
   Until she espied his cloven foot,
   And she wept right bitterlie.

14 'O hold your tongue of your weeping,' says he,
   ' Of your weeping now let me be;
   I will show you how the lilies grow
   On the banks of Italy.'

15 'O what hills are yon, yon pleasant hills,
   That the sun shines sweetly on?
   'O yon are the hills of heaven,' he said,
   'Where you will never win.'

16 'O whaten a mountain is yon,' she said,
   'All so dreary wi' frost and snow?'
   'O yon is the mountain of hell,' he cried,
   'Where you and I will go.'

17 And aye when she turn'd her round about,
   Aye taller he seem'd for to be;

Until that the tops o' that gallant ship
    Nae taller were than he.

18 The clouds grew dark, and the wind grew loud,
    And the levin fill'd her ee;
And waesome wail'd the snaw-white sprites
    Upon the gurlie sea.

19 He struck the tapmast wi' his hand,
    The foremast wi' his knee;
And he brak that gallant ship in twain,
    And sank her in the sea.

THE DEMON LOVER
[From Andrew Lang, *Border Ballads*, pp. 41-43.]

'O where have you been, my long-lost love,
    This long seven years and mair?'
'O I'm come to seek my former vows,
    Ye granted me before.'

'O hold your tongue of your former vows,
    For they will breed sad strife;
O hold your tongue of your former vows,
    For I am become a wife.'

He turn'd him right and round about,
    And the tear blinded his e'e:
'I wad never hae trodden on Irish ground,
    If it had not been for thee.

'I might have had a king's daughter,
    Far, far beyond the sea;
I might have had a king's daughter,
    Had it not been for love o' thee.'

'If ye might have had a king's daughter,
    Yersel ye had to blame;
Ye might have taken the king's daughter,
    For ye kend that I was nane.'

'O faulse are the vows o' womankind,
    But fair is their faulse bodie;

I never wad hae trodden on Irish ground,
    Had it not been for love o' thee.'

'If I was to leave my husband dear,
    And my two babes also,
O what have you to take me to,
    If with you I should go?'

'I have seven ships upon the sea,
    The eighth brought me to land;
With four-and-twenty bold mariners,
    And music on every hand.'

She has taken up her two little babes,
    Kiss'd them baith cheek and chin;
'O fare ye weel, my ain twa babes,
    For I'll never see you again.'

She set her foot upon the ship,
    No mariners could she behold;
But the sails were o' the taffetie
    And the masts o' the beaten gold

They had not sail'd a league, a league,
    A league but barely three,
Until she espied his cloven foot,
    And she wept right bitterlie.

'O hold your tongue of your weeping,' says he,
    'Of your weeping now let me be;
I will show you how the lilies grow
    On the banks of Italy.'

'O what hills are yon, yon pleasant hills,
    That the sun shines sweetly on?'
'O yon are the hills of heaven,' he said,
    'Where you will never win.'

'O whaten a mountain is yon,' she said,
    'All so dreary wi' frost and snow?'
'O yon is the mountain of hell,' he cried,
    'Where you and I will go.'

And aye when she turn'd her round about,
    Aye taller he seem'd to be;
Until that the tops o' the gallant ship
    Nae taller were than he.

He strack the tapmast wi' his hand,
   The foremast wi' his knee;
And he brake that gallant ship in twain,
   And sank her in the sea.


## THE DEMON LOVER

Sir Walter Scott first printed this ballad, having received
it from Mr. William Laidlaw, who took it down from
recitation. Motherwell subsequently recovered a fragment of the same legend, and Buchan, in his "Ballads of
the North of Scotland," gives another version of the present poem, under the title of "James Herries." [From
George Barnett Smith, ed., *Illustrated British Ballads, Old
and New*, pp. 143-45.]

   "O  where have you been, my long, long love,
      This long seven years and more?"
   "O I'm come to seek my former vows
   Ye granted me before."

   "O hold your tongue of your former vows,
      For they will breed sad strife;
   O hold your tongue of your former vows,
      For I am become a wife."

   He turned him right and round about,
      And the tear blinded his ee.
   "I wad never hae trodden on Irish ground,
      If it had not been for thee.

   "I might hae had a king's daughtèr,
      Far, far beyond the sea;
   I might have had a king's daughtèr,
      Had it not been for love o' thee."

   "If ye might have had a king's daughtèr,
      Yer sell ye had to blame;
   Ye might have taken the king's daughtèr,
      For ye ken'd that I was nane."

   "O fause are the vows of womankind,
      But fair is their fause bodie;
   I never wad hae trod on Irish ground,
      Had it not been for love o' thee."

"If I was to leave my husband dear,
  And my two babes also,
O what have you to take me to,
  If with you I should go?"

"I hae seven ships upon the sea,
  The eighth brought me to land;
With four-and-twenty bold marinèrs,
  And music on every hand."

She had taken up her two little babes,
  Kiss'd them baith cheek and chin;
"O fare ye weel, my ain two babes,
  For I'll never see you again."

She set her foot upon the ship
  No mariners could she behold;
But the sails were o' the taffetie,
  And the masts o' the beaten gold.

She had not sail'd a league, a league,
  A league but barely three,
When dismal grew his countenance,
  And drumlie grew his ee.

The masts that were like the beaten gold
  Bent not on the heaving seas,
And the sails that were o' the taffetie,
  Fill'd not in the east land breeze.

They had not sail'd a league, a league,
  A league but barely three,
Until she espied his cloven foot,
  And she wept right bitterlie.

"O hold your tongue of your weeping," says he,
  "Of your weeping now let me be;
I will show you how the lilies grow
  On the banks of Italy."

"O what hills are yon, yon pleasant hills,
  That the sun shines sweetly on?"
"O yon are the hills of heaven." he said,
  Where you will never win."

"O whatten a mountain is yon," she said,
  "All so dreary wi' frost and snow?"

"O yon is the mountain of hell," he cried,
  "Where you and I will go."

And aye when she turned her round about,
  Aye taller he seem'd for to be,
Until that the tops o' that gallant ship
  Nae taller were than he.

The clouds grew dark, and the wind grew loud,
  And the levin fill'd her ee;
And waesome wail'd the snaw-white sprites
  Upon the gurlie sea.

He strack the tap-mast wi' his hand,
  The fore-mast wi' his knee;
And he brake that gallant ship in twain.
  And sank her in the sea.

# NOTES

1. In an unpublished dissertation, "Demon Lovers: The Myth of Psyche in the Development of the Romantic Novel," Wayne Douglas Batten recognizes the prevalence of the demon-lover as a mythical figure, and attributes the inception of the myth to Apuleius' *The Golden Ass*. Batten makes passing reference to "The Demon Lover" ballad, although he mistakenly attributes Francis James Child's important work *The English and Scottish Popular Ballads* to Francis James Harris, thinking no doubt of an early version of the ballad, entitled "James Harris." Batten fails to recognize the complexity of the ballad's influence upon demon-lover tales, implying that there exists one particular text of the ballad which reflects the myth focused upon in his work. It is important to point out, however, that at least two hundred and fifty versions of the ballad have been collected, and, as with any comparative approach, a thorough analysis must be made of the ballads themselves before making statements regarding the ballad's impact upon a body of literature. Chapter 3 of this book presents such an analysis.

2. Interestingly, in many works of pornography and erotica (works by the Marquis de Sade, for example), a whip unmistakably symbolizes masculine power and domination over women.

3. For the remainder of this discussion I shall refer to witches as women.

4. Closely connected with the noun *śātān* is *mastēmā*, an evil spirit recognized as a devil in late Judaism; Mastema essentially played the same role as Satan in the Old Testament (Kluger, p. 28).

5. Many scholars, including Jules Michelet and Jeffrey Burton Russell, believe that women were *compelled* to "confess."

6. For a fuller discussion of the dissemination of ballads, see Archer Taylor's classic study *"Edward" and "Sven I Rosengard": A Study in the Dissemination of a Ballad*.

7. Surviving examples of any ballad, both those found in oral tradition and those written down at any point in history, represent a minute portion of that ballad's evolutionary path. Examining a finite corpus of ballad texts in an attempt to comprehend fully the history of that ballad is akin to experiencing an hour of time and generalizing about the entire century in which the hour falls. Thus, this study, as any study of textual evolution, is necessarily limited by the relatively few versions that have come down to us.

8. This tune has not survived. In *The Traditional Tunes of The Child Ballad*, Bertrand Harris Bronson presents numerous tune variants for the ballad entitled "The Daemon Lover" or alternatively "The Ship Carpenter" or "The

House Carpenter," identifying the tunes by the titles rather than by separate tune directions. Tunes vary as often as the lyrics in Bronson's collection. Claude M. Simpson identifies the tune "I am James Harris call'd by name, or Ladies Fall," catalogued as 4to Rawlinson 566 in the Rawlinson collection located in the Bodleian Library. As Simpson points out, the first tune name approximates two lines from "A Warning for Married Women" (*The British Broadside Ballad and Its Music*, p. 370).

9. According to Leslie Shepard, "In 1533 a proclamation was issued for the suppression of 'fond books, ballads, rhimes, and other lewd treatises in the English tongue' " (*The Broadside Ballad: A Study in Origins and Meanings*, p. 51). And in 1543, an act was passed "for the advancement of true religion, and for the abolishment of the contrary," meaning ballads, rhymes, and songs that were thought to subvert scripture and thus to corrupt the people (p. 52). By 1520, broadsides accounted for a large portion of the provincial booksellers' sales, and approximately forty printers registered ballads with the Stationer's Company during the early years of Queen Elizabeth's reign (1553-1603) (Friedman, p. 46).

10. According to H.E. Rollins, a listing for the earliest version, "A Warning for Married Women," is dated 1657, which indicates that the ballad existed at least twenty-eight years before Pepys is said to have collected his version.

11. Estimates vary, but the number of people executed in Europe for witchcraft between 1484 and the middle of the eighteenth century is perhaps between 30,000 and nine million, according to Mary Daly, who cites Matilda Joslyn Gage, Felix Morrow's foreword to Montague Summers, *The History of Witchcraft and Demonology*, and Rossell Hope Robbins (*Gyn/Ecology; The Metaethics of Radical Feminism*, p. 183).

12. For a fuller discussion of supernatural elements in Anglo-American ballad variants, see Bill Ellis's "I Wonder, Wonder, Mother': Death and the Angels in Native American Balladry," *Western Folklore* 38 (1979): 170-85.

13. Scott's version is included in Child's anthology and identified as "F." Throughout this discussion, however, I shall refer to the version as Scott's rather than Child F because the two versions are distinctly different. Believing that Scott had tampered with his text, Child "corrected" certain features of the version; for example, Child omitted three stanzas and made slight orthographic and punctuation changes. However, Scott's version as it appeared in *Minstrelsy* influenced the history of the ballad as shown by similar versions later printed in popular songbooks. In his *Illustrated British Ballads, Old and New* (1881), George Barnett Smith duplicated Scott's version more or less faithfully, citing Scott as his source. Andrew Lang alters Scott's version in *Border Ballads* (1895), but he does retain one of Scott's intrusive stanzas (" 'O faulse are the vows of womankind"), a stanza subsequently included in a number of nineteenth-century songbooks (see Appendix C).

14. George Barnett Smith's *Illustrated British Ballads, Old and New* (1881), the anonymous collection *The Ballad Minstrelsy of Scotland* (1893), Andrew Lang's *Border Ballads* (1895), and several others all include versions with this feature.

15. Many American versions retain the image of the mountains of heaven and hell as well.

16. In an earlier text, Child B, once at sea the woman cries for the children she left behind, an element included in most of the later versions.

17. Although some two hundred and fifty versions of "The Demon Lover" are known to exist, this comparison is restricted to the seven Child versions and the first seven versions presented by Arthur Kyle Davis, Jr.

18. Kiessling adds the following note to this discussion: "*De Divortio Lotharii*, Interrog. 15 (PL 125,725). C. Grant Loomis, *White Magic* (Cambridge, Mass., 1948), lists later stories of the demon molester found in the *Acta Sactorum*, see pp. 77 and 187, note 140" (p. 92).

19. The tremendous popularity of Harlequin Romances (a spin-off form of Gothic fiction) among contemporary readers cannot be denied. According to Tania Modleski in *Loving With a Vengeance: Mass-Produced Fantasies for Women*, "The success of Harlequin Enterprises, Ltd., which is based in Toronto, has been extraordinary. Since 1958 when the first Harlequin Romance was published, over 2,300 titles have appeared. In 1977, Harlequin had 10 percent of the paperback market in North America, selling 100 million books on this continent and 50 million more in countries like Israel, Germany, and Holland" (p. 35).

20. According to "A Note on Authorship" in the Dover Edition of *Varney the Vampyre or The Feast of Blood*, there has been critical debate regarding the authorship of this work; some believe that Rymer wrote the novel, while others believe the author to be one Thomas Peckett Prest. To determine authorship, the publisher conducted several stylistic analyses and concludes that Rymer is the author by virtue of the minimal number of synonyms employed for the word "said" during passages of dialogue (pp. xvii-xviii).

21. See, for example, "Lord Thomas and Fair Annet" (Child 73), "Fair Margaret and Sweet William" (Child 74), or "Lord Lovel" (Child 75).

22. A footnote in the Penguin edition cites Shakespeare's *Rape of Lucrece*, l. 871, as the source of the original line, "The adder hisses where the sweet birds sing" (p. 526).

23. Referring to F.B. Pinion's *Thomas Hardy: Art and Thought*, Dale Kramer states: "Pinion makes a strong case for an influence on the design of *Tess of the d'Urbervilles* by Richardson's *Clarissa*, a novel Hardy had read and admired in 1888, not long before he began to write his novel. One of the verbal similarities he identifies is between 'Once subdued, always subdued' in *Clarissa* and 'Once victim, always victim—that's the law!' in *Tess of the d'Urbervilles*" (pp. 138-39).

24. The aggressor/victim interaction in the ballad identifies one type of configuration possible for the psyche; there are others. Jung's concept of the "Mother archetype," for example, is demonstrated metaphorically by ballads such as "Fair Annie" and "Child Waters," and "the negative mother-complex" is presented by ballads such as "Lord Randal." I am grateful to Ann C. Hall for sharing with me her unpublished paper "A Jungian Interpretation of 'Lord Randal' or 'What was worse than woman was?' "

25. For a fuller discussion of the critical debate surrounding the scene in the Chase, see H.M. Daleski, *"Tess of the d'Urbervilles*: Mastery and Abandon,"* J.T. Laird claims that Hardy intended his readers to conclude that Alec actually rapes Tess; he identifies telling revisions in the 1892 edition to support his belief (*The Shaping of "Tess of the D'Urbervilles,"* pp. 174-79).

26. The American film *Fatal Attraction* is one of the few literary examples of a female demon-lover. The fact that most demon-lover tales involve male rather than female demon-lovers lends further support for the idea that these works reflect the domination and oppression of women which take place daily within patriarchal societies.

27. In a footnote, Peck remarks, "Jung correctly ascribed evil to the failure to 'meet' the Shadow" (p. 69).

28. For further psychological exploration of victimizers and victims, see *Sweet Suffering: Woman as Victim*, by Natalie Shainess, and *Men Who Hate Women and the Women Who Love Them*, by Susan Forward and Joan Torres.

29. See Richardson's letter to Lady Dorothy Bradshaigh, 15 December 1748 (J. Carroll, ed., *Selected Letters of Samuel Richardson*, p. 104). In *The Shaping of "Tess of the D'Urbervilles,"* Laird quotes from a letter to Hardy held at the Dorcet County Museum in Dorchester, England, in which Edward Arnold, editor of *Murray's Magazine*, rejects *Tess* as inappropriate for his magazine; "I know your views are different, and I honour your motive, which is, as you told me, to spare many girls the misery of unhappy marriages made in ignorance of how wicked men can be" (p. 10).

# WORKS CITED

Abrahams, Roger D., and George Foss. *Anglo-American Folksong Style.*
    Englewood Cliffs, N.J.: Prentice, 1968.
Auerbach, Nina. *Woman and the Demon: The Life of a Victorian Myth.*
    Cambridge: Harvard UP, 1982.
Austin, Allen E. *Elizabeth Bowen.* N.Y.: Twayne, 1971.
Ballad Minstrelsy, The. London: Alexander Gardner, 1893.
Barnett, W.F. "Satan." *The New Catholic Encyclopedia.* Washington,
    D.C.: The Catholic U. of America, 1967.
Batten, Wayne Douglas. "Demon Lovers: The Myth of Psyche in the
    Development of the Romantic Novel." Diss. Vanderbilt U, 1983.
Bayer-Berenbaum, Linda. *The Gothic Imagination: Expansion in Gothic
    Literature and Art.* East Brunswick, N.J.: Associated UP, 1982.
Becker, George J. *D.H. Lawrence.* New York: Frederick Ungar, 1980.
Bentley, C.F. "The Monster in the Bedroom: Sexual Symbolism in
    Bram Stoker's *Dracula.*" *Literature and Psychology* 22 (1972): 27-34.
Bodkin, Maud. *Archetypal Patterns in Poetry: Psychological Studies of
    Imagination.* New York: Oxford UP, 1934.
Bowen, Elizabeth. "The Demon Lover." *The Collected Stories of Eliza-
    beth Bowen.* New York: Knopf, 1981.
———. *Collected Impressions* London: Longmans Green, 1950.
Bronson, Bertrand Harris. *The Traditional Tunes of The Child Ballad:
    With Their Texts, According to the Extant Records of Great Britain and
    America.* Princeton: Princeton UP, 1966.
Brontë, Charlotte. *Jane Eyre.* 1847; rpt. New York: Norton, 1971.
Brontë, Emily. *Wuthering Heights.* 1847; rpt. New York: Norton, 1972.
Brownmiller, Susan. *Against Our Will: Men, Women and Rape.* New
    York: Bantam, 1976.
Buchan, David. *The Ballad and the Folk.* London: Routledge and Kegan
    Paul, 1972.
Buchan, Peter, ed. *Ancient Ballads and Songs of the North of Scotland.*
    1828; rpt. Edinburgh: William Paterson, 1875.
———. *Ballads of the North of Scotland.* Edinburgh, 1828.
Burrison, John. " 'James Harris' in Britain since Child." *Journal of
    American Folklore* 80 (Jul.-Sept. 1967): 271-84.

Carroll, John J., ed. *Selected Letters of Samuel Richardson.* Oxford: Clarendon, 1964.

Cavendish, Richard. *The Powers of Evil in Western Religion, Magic and Folk Belief.* London: Routledge and Kegan Paul, 1975.

Chase, Richard. *Quest for Myth.* Baton Rouge: Louisiana State UP, 1949.

Child, Francis James, ed. *The English and Scottish Popular Ballads.* 5 vols. 1882-1898; rpt. New York:. Dover, 1965.

Coffin, Tristram P. *The British Traditional Ballad in North America.* Rev. ed. Philadelphia: American Folklore Society, 1963.

*Collection of Old Ballads, A.* 3 vols. London, 1723-1725.

Daleski, H.M. "*Tess of the D'Urbervilles*: Mastery and Abandon." *Essays in Criticism* 30 (Oct. 1980): 326-45.

Daly, Mary. *Gym/Ecology: The Metaethics of Radical Feminism.* Boston: Beacon, 1978.

Davidson, Donald. "The Traditional Basis of Thomas Hardy's Fiction." *Hardy: A Collection of Critical Essays.* Ed. Albert Guerard. Englewood Cliffs, N.J.: Prentice, 1963.

Davis, Arthur Kyle, Jr. *Traditional Ballads of Virginia.* 1929; rpt. Charlottesville: UP of Virginia, 1969.

de Bruyn, Lucy. *Woman and the Devil in Sixteenth-Century Literature.* Tisbury, Wiltshire, Eng.: Compton, 1979.

Drake, Carlos C. "Jungian Psychology and Its Uses in Folklore." *Journal of American Folklore* 82 (Apr.-June 1969): 122-31.

Draper, Ronald P. *D.H. Lawrence.* New York: Twayne, 1964.

Eagleton, Terry. *The Rape of Clarissa: Writing, Sexuality, and Class Struggle in Samuel Richardson.* Minneapolis: U of Minnesota, 1982.

Ellis, Bill. "'I Wonder, Wonder, Mother': Death and the Angels in Native American Balladry." *Western Folklore* 38 (1979): 170-85.

Fiedler, Leslie A. *Love and Death in the American Novel.* New York: Stein and Day, 1965.

Forward, Susan, and Joan Torres. *Men Who Hate Women and the Women Who Love Them.* 1986. New York: Bantam Books, 1987.

Fowles, John. *The Collector.* New York: Little, Brown, 1963.

———. *The French Lieutenant's Woman.* New York: Little, Brown, 1969.

Fraustino, Daniel V. "Elizabeth Bowen's 'The Demon Lover': Psychosis or Seduction?" *Studies in Short Fiction* 17 (1980): 483-87.

Friedman, Albert B. *The Ballad Revival: Studies in the Influence of Popular on Sophisticated Poetry.* Chicago: U of Chicago P, 1961.

Fromm, Erich. *The Anatomy of Human Destructiveness.* Greenwich, Conn.: Fawcett, 1973.

Frye, Northrop. *Anatomy of Criticism*. Princeton: Princeton UP, 1957.

Gage, Matilda Joslyn. *Woman, Church and State*. 2nd ed. New York: Arno, 1972.

Gardner-Medwin, Alisoun. "The Ancestry of 'The House-Carpenter': A Study of the Family History of the American Forms of Child 243." *Journal of American Folklore* 84 (Oct.-Dec. 1971): 414-27.

Gerould, Gordon Hall. *The Ballad of Tradition*. New York: Oxford UP, 1932.

Gibb, Ellen-Monica. "Thomas Hardy's Use of Traditional English Ballad Form in *Far from the Madding Crowd*." *Papers in Comparative Studies* 2 (1983): 187-205.

Gilbert, Sandra M., and Susan Gubar. *The Madwoman in the Attic: The Woman Writer and the Nineteenth-Century Literary Imagination.* New Haven, Conn.: Yale UP, 1979.

Gould, Eric. *Mythical Intentions in Modern Literature*. Princeton: Princeton UP, 1981.

Gummere, Francis B. *Old English Ballads*. Boston, 1894.

Hafley, James. "The Villain of *Wuthering Heights*." *Nineteenth-Century Fiction* 13 (1958): 199-215.

Hall, Ann C. "A Jungian Interpretation of 'Lord Randal,' or 'What was worse than woman was?' " Unpublished essay, 1983.

Hardwick, Elizabeth. *Seduction and Betrayal: Women and Literature*. New York: Random House, 1970.

Hardy, Thomas. *Tess of the d'Urbervilles: A Pure Woman*. 1891; rpt. New York: Penguin, 1979.

Hatlen, Burton. "The Return of the Repressed/Oppressed in Bram Stoker's *Dracula*." *Minnesota Review* 15 (1980): 80-97.

Herd, David. *Ancient and Modern Scottish Songs*. 2 vols. Edinburgh, 1776.

Hodgart, M.J.C. *The Ballads*. London: Hutchinson's, 1950.

Holt, Victoria. *The Demon Lover*. New York: Doubleday, 1982.

Howells, Coral Ann. *Love, Mystery, and Misery: Feeling in Gothic Fiction*. London: Athlone, 1978.

Hughes, Douglas A. "Cracks in the Psyche: Elizabeth Bowen's "The Demon Lover.' " *Studies in Short Fiction* 10 (1973): 411-13.

Jameson, Frederick. "Magical Narratives: Romance as Genre." *New Literary History* 7 (1975): 135-63.

Jung, C.G. *Aion: Researches into the Phenomenology of the Self*. Trans. R.F.C. Hull. New York: Pantheon, 1959.

———. *Contributions to Analytical Psychology*. Trans. H.G. and Cary F. Baynes. New York: Harcourt, 1928.

158        *Works Cited*

———. *Four Archetypes: Mother, Rebirth, Spirit, Trickster*. Trans. R.F.C. Hull. Princeton: Princeton UP, 1970.

———. *The Spirit in Man, Art, and Literature*. Trans. R.F.C. Hull. 1966; Princeton: Princeton UP, 1971.

———. *Two Essays on Analytical Psychology*. 2nd ed. Trans. R.F.C. Hull. New York: Pantheon, 1966.

Keith, Alexander. "Scottish Ballads: Their Evidence of Authorship and Origin." *English Association Essays and Studies*, 1926: xii, 100-119.

Kiessling, Nicolas K. "Demonic Dread: The Incubus Figure in British Literature." *The Gothic Imagination: Essays in Dark Romanticism*. Ed. G.R. Thompson. Pullman: Washington State UP, 1974.

———. *The Incubus in English Literature: Provenance and Progeny*. Pullman: Washington State UP, 1977.

Klingopulos, G.D. "The Novel as Dramatic Poem (II): 'Wuthering Heights.' " *Scrutiny* 14 (1946-1947).

Kluger, Rivkah Schärf. *Satan in the Old Testament*. Trans. Hildegard Nagel. Evanston: Northwestern UP, 1967.

Kramer, Dale. *Critical Approaches to the Fiction of Thomas Hardy*. London: Macmillan, 1979.

Laird, J.T. *The Shaping of "Tess of the D'Urbervilles."* Oxford: Clarendon, 1975.

Lang, Andrew. *Border Ballads*. London: Lawrence and Bullen; New York: Longman's, 1895.

Lawrence, D.H. "The Princess" *The Complete Short Stories*. New York: Viking, 1961.

———. *Women in Love*. 1920; rpt. New York: Penguin, 1976.

Laws, G. Malcolm. *American Balladry from British Broadsides: A Guide for Students and Collectors of Traditional Song*. Philadelphia: American Folklore Society, 1957.

———. *The British Literary Ballad: A Study in Poetic Imitation*. Carbondale: Southern Illinois UP, 1972.

———. *Native American Balladry: A Descriptive Study and a Bibliographical Syllabus*. Philadelphia: American Folklore Society, 1964.

Leach, MacEdward, and Tristram P. Coffin, eds. *The Critics and the Ballad*. Carbondale: Southern Illinois UP, 1961.

Lessing, Doris. *The Four-Gated City*. New York: Knopf, 1969.

Loomis, C. Grant. *White Magic*. Cambridge: Harvard UP, 1948.

MacAndrew, Elizabeth. *The Gothic Tradition in Fiction*. New York: Columbia UP, 1979.

May, Rollo. *Love and Will*. New York: Norton, 1969.

Works Cited            159

Michelet, Jules. *Satanism and Witchcraft: A Study in Medieval Supersti-tion.* Trans. A.R. Allinson. 1939; rpt. New York: Citadel, 1960.

Modleski, Tania. *Loving with a Vengeance: Mass-Produced Fantasies for Women.* New York: Methuen, 1982.

Morrow, Felix. Foreword to *The History of Witchcraft and Demonology,* by Montague Summers. Secaucus, N.J.: Citadel, 1971.

Motherwell, William. *Minstrelsy, Ancient and Modern.* 2 vols. Glasgow, 1827.

Norwood, Robin. *Women Who Love Too Much: When You Keep Wishing and Hoping He'll Change.* Los Angeles: Tarcher, 1985.

Peck, M. Scott. *People of the Lie: The Hope for Healing Human Evil.* New York: Simon, 1983.

Peele, Stanton. *Love and Addiction.* New York: Taplinger, 1975.

Percy, Thomas. *Reliques of Ancient English Poetry.* Ed. Henry B. Wheatley. 3 vols. London, 1886.

Pinion, F.B. *Thomas Hardy: Art and Thought.* London: Macmillan; Totowa, N.J.: Rowman and Littlefield, 1977.

Pratt, Annis. "Archetypal Approaches to the New Feminist Criticism." *Bucknell Review* 21 (1973): 3-14.

———. *Archetypal Patterns in Women's Fiction.* Bloomington: Indiana UP, 1981.

Railo, Eino. *The Haunted Castle: A Study of the Elements of English Romanticism.* London: Routledge; New York: Dutton, 1927.

Ramsay, Allan. *The Ever Green: A Collection of Scots Poems Wrote by the Ingenious before 1600.* 2 vols. Edinburgh, 1724; rpt. 1874.

———. *Tea-Table Miscellany, The.* 1723-1737; rpt., 2 vols., Glasgow: Robert Forrester, 1876.

Remy, Nicolas. *Demonolatry.* Ed. John Rodker. London: Rodker, 1930.

Richardson, Samuel. *Clarissa; or, The History of a Young Lady.* London, 1747-1748.

Robbins, Rossell Hope. *The Encyclopedia of Witchcraft and Demonology.* New York: Crown, 1959.

Robinson, Lillian S. "Dwelling in Decencies: Radical Criticism and the Feminist Perspective." *Feminist Criticism: Essays on Theory, Poetry and Prose.* Ed. Cheryl L. Brown and Karen Olson. Metuchen, N.J.: Scarecrow, 1978.

Rollins, H.E. "An Analytical Index to the Ballad Entries in the Registers of the Company of Stationers." *Studies in Philology* 21 (1924): 1-324.

*Roxburghe Ballads, The.* 9 vols. 1875; rpt. New York: AMS Press, 1966.

Russell, Jeffrey Burton. *The Devil: Perceptions of Evil from Antiquity to Primitive Christianity*. Ithaca: Cornell UP, 1977.

Rymer, James Malcolm. *Varney the Vampire or The Feast of Blood*. 1847; rpt., 2 vols., New York: Dover, 1972.

Scott, Sir Walter. *Minstrelsy of the Scottish Border*. 4 vols., 1802-1803; rpt., ed. T.F. Henderson, New York: Scribners, 1902.

Shainess, Natalie. *Sweet Suffering: Woman as Victim*. 1984. New York: Pocket Books, 1986.

Shepard, Leslie. *The Broadside Ballad: A Study in Origins and Meanings*. London: Herbert Jenkins, 1962.

Simpson, Claude M. *The British Broadside Ballad and Its Music*. New Brunswick, N.J.: Rutgers UP, 1966.

Smith, George Barnett, ed. *Illustrated British Ballads, Old and New*. 2 vols. London: Cassell, Petter, Golpin, 1881. Vol. 1.

Stern, Paul J. *In Praise of Madness: Realness Therapy—The Self Reclaimed*. New York: Norton, 1972.

Stimpson, Catharine R. "Introduction." *Feminist Issues in Literary Scholarship*, ed. Shari Benstock. Bloomington: Indiana UP, 1987.

Stoker, Bram. *Dracula*. 1897; rpt. New York: Bantam, 1981.

Styron, William. *Sophie's Choice*. New York: Random, 1979.

Summers, Montague. *The History of Witchcraft and Demonology*. Secaucus, N.J.: Citadel, 1971.

———. *The Vampire: His Kith and Kin*. New York: University Books, 1960.

Taylor, Archer. *"Edward" and "Sven I Rosengard": A Study in the Dissemination of a Ballad*. Chicago: U of Chicago P, 1931.

Thompson, G.R., ed. *The Gothic Imagination: Essays in Dark Romanticism*. Pullman: Washington State UP, 1974.

Thompson, Stith. *The Folktale*. 1946; rpt. Berkeley: U of California P, 1977.

Twitchell, James. "Heathcliff as Vampire." *Southern Humanities Review* 11 (1977): 355-62.

Van Ghent, Dorothy. *The English Novel: Form and Function*. 1953. New York: Harper 1961.

Veitch, John. *The History and Poetry of the Scottish Border*. 2 vols. Edinburgh: Blackwood, 1893.

Wehr, Demaris S. "Religious and Social Dimensions of Jung's Concept of the Archetype: A Feminist Perspective." In *Feminist Archetypal Theory: Interdisciplinary Re-Visions of Jungian Thought*, ed. Estella Lauter and Carol Schreier Rupprecht, pp. 23-45. Knoxville: U. of Tennessee P., 1985.

Weissman, Judith. "Woman and Vampires: *Dracula* as a Victorian Novel." *Midwestern Quarterly* 18 (1977): 392-405.

Wells, Evelyn Kendrick. *The Ballad Tree: A Study of British and American Ballads, Their Folklore, Verse, and Music.* New York: Ronald Press, 1950.

White, John J. "Mythological Fiction and the Reading Process." *Literary Criticism and Myth.* Ed. Joseph P. Strelka. University Park: Pennsylvania State UP, 1980.

Widmer, Kingsley. *The Art of Perversity: D. H. Lawrence's Shorter Fictions.* Seattle: U of Washington P, 1962.

# INDEX

Abrahams, Roger D., 42
"absurd criminal," 107
addiction, 115
aggression, 99, 117; in Bowen's
  "Demon Lover," 7, 87; in *Clarisa*,
  7; in *Dance with a Stranger*, 102; in
  "Demon Lover" ballad, 99; of demon-lovers, 103, 110; human, 18,
  104-5; in "The Princess," 7;
  sexual, 62, 106; in *Tess*, 7; and victimization, 153 n 24; in *Wuthering
  Heights*, 7. *See also* rape victimization
alienation, 104
"angel in the House," 9, 12
angels, 12, 25, 29
*anima*, 14-15, 19
*animus*, 14-15, 19
Apollo, 23
Apuleius, 151 n 1
Aquinas, Thomas, 31
archetypal criticism, 6. *See also*
  myth criticism
archetype: archetypal literature, 7; in
  ballads, 98; characters as, 14; demon-lover, 15, 17; gender-linked,
  6, 14. *See also* Bodkin, Maud; Frye,
  Northrop; Jung, C.G.
Aristotle, 3, 7
Arnold, Edward, 154 n 29
Auerbach, Nina, 12
Austen, Jane: *Pride and Prejudice*,
  11-12
Austin, Allen E., 87

ballads, 3, 6, 38, 55, 75, 76, 77, 92;
  American and British versions of,

42; Black-Letter, 37; characteristics
  of, 69; dating and origins of, 35,
  38; effect of collections on, 39-40;
  Emily Brontë and, 69; evolution
  of, 39-40; history of, 42, 52, 151
  n 7; supernatural in, 35, 40-42,
  152 n 12; suppression of, 152 n 9;
  tampering with, 39. *See also*
  broadsides; Child ballads; *ballads
  by name*
Batten, Wayne Douglas, 151 n 1
Bayer-Berenbaum, Linda, 57-59
Becker, George J., 80
Bentley, C.F., 61
Blakely, David, 102
Bodkin, Maud, 6, 8
Boquet, Henri, 27
Bowen, Elizabeth, 7, 80, 89, 91,
  100, 101, 103, 114; *Collected Impressions*, 91; *Collected Stories*, 88;
  "Preface" to *The Demon Lovers*, 91
—"The Demon Lover," 87, 100,
  114; as contemporary demon-
  lover ballad, 91; demon-lover motif in, 91-92; and "Demon Lover"
  ballad, 53, 88; motivation in,
  108; as supernatural tale, 87;
  vow in, 89, 91. *See also characters
  by name*
Bradshaigh, Lady Dorothy, 154
  n 29
broadsides, 36-40; influence on orally transmitted ballads, 39
Bronson, Bertrand Harris, 151-52
  n 8
Brontë, Charlotte, 9, 68, 101, 107;
  *Jane Eyre*, 9, 101

Brontë, Emily, vii, 11, 13, 15, 68, 70, 71, 81, 100, 107; and ballads, 74; and evil, 92; and ghosts, 73; influence of "Demon Lover" ballad on, 16; and obsession, 75 —*Wuthering Heights*, 4, 70, 75, 99; and ballads, 69-70, 74; and "Demon Lover" ballad, 7, 33, 53, 68, 70, 75, 100, 103, 114; demon-lover conflict in, 100; devil in, 74, 75; as film, 101; motivation in, 108; obsession in, 69, 75, 100; passion in, 8, 11; Pratt on, 10-11; vampirization in, 74; Van Ghent on, 15; vow in, 71. *See also characters by name*
Brownmiller, Susan, 106
Buchan, Peter, 46, 47, 51
Byron, Lord, 60

Cather, Willa, 101
Cavendish, Richard, 26, 31, 32
chapbooks, 37
Chase, Richard, 4-5
"Chevy Chase," 69
Child, Francis James, 22, 36, 38, 40, 152 n 13; *English and Scottish Popular Ballads*, 22, 38, 40, 151 n 1
Child ballads, 33, 35, 40, 47. *See also by name*
"Child Waters," 47
Christ, 66
Claire, Angel (*Tess*), 76, 77, 78, 80
Coffin, Tristram P., 52, 55
*Collection of Old Ballads, A* (anon.), 37-38
"collective unconscious," 54, 99
"communal recreation," 42-43
conflict: archetypal, 12; between victimizer and victim, 16; demon-lover, viii, 3, 17; empowerment through, 12; and sexuality, 24
Cummins, Miss ("The Princess"), 83-85

Daly, Mary, 152 n 11
*Dance with a Stranger* (film), 102
Davidson, Donald, 77
Davis, Arthur Kyle, Jr.: ballad texts, 22, 47, 133-43, 153 n 17
Dean, Nelly (*Wuthering Heights*), 70-74, 99; as villain, 70
death: desire for, 8; and Gothic literature, 59; and sexuality, 17, 24, 65, 106
de Bruyn, Lucy, 30
de Lancre, Pierre, 27
demon(s), 52, 74, 108; in ballads, 42; belief in, 41; in Bowen's "Demon Lover," 91; classification system, King James's, 30; in "Demon Lover" ballad, 22, 44, 91; as *familiars* for witches, 31; in Gothic literature, 57; Greek, 30; as incubi and succubi, 31; as lovers, 7, 22, 55; as mytholigical figures, 5; names and number of, 30; offspring of, 31; in "The Princess," 82, 84, 87; and sexuality, 13-14, 29, 31, 108; and sleep, 31; tales of, 54; and witches, 29. *See also* devil(s)
"Demon Lover, The" (ballad), 2, 4, 7, 42, 69, 80, 90, 99, 101, 151 n 1, 153 n 17; *anima* and *animus* in, 14-15; and belief in vampires, 60; and Bowen's "Demon Lover," 88; characters in, 44, 45, 47, 151 n 1; comparison of Pepys's version with Scott's, 43-46; complex, 16-17; core characteristics of, 34; demon-lover in, 54; demon-lover conflict in, 104; demon-lover motif in, 103; and demon-lover tales, 17, 117; and *Dracula*, 65; "emotional core" of, 52, 55; families of, 46-47, 48-50; and Gothic literature, 57; influence of Scott's *Minstrelsy* on, 152 n 13; and literature, 20-21, 33, 68, 70, 92, 98; lover as

God, 112

Gothic literature, 58; British tradition of, 18, 52; fiction, 55, 57-59, 102-3, 153 n 19; characteristics of, 55-59; and "Demon Lover" ballad, 57; and death, 59; popularity of, 55; readers of, 57; and religion, 58; romances, 55; supernatural in, 58; tales, 62

Gould, Eric, 5

Greek mythology, 2, 10, 23, 24

Greeks, 24

"Green-world," 10, 11, 12

Gubar, Susan, 9

Gummere, Francis B., 42-43

Hafley, James, 70

Hall, Ann C., 153 n 24

Hardwick, Elizabeth, 106

Hardy, Thomas, vii, 16, 68, 75, 81, 92, 100, 103, 116, 153 n 23; *Far from the Madding Crowd*, 77 —*Tess of the d'Urbervilles*, 4, 53, 114; ballads in, 75-77; and "Demon Lover" ballad, 33, 75-76, 78; demon-lover conflict in, 100; demon-lover motif in, 7, 68; as demon-lover tale, 80; as film, 101; influence of *Clarissa* on, 153 n 23; motivation in, 108; obsession in, 69, 79; rape in, 78, 100, 154 n 25; violence in, 106; as warning, 116, 154 n 29. *See also characters by name*

Harker, Jonathan (*Dracula*), 65

Harker, Mina (*Dracula*), 61, 64

Harlequin Romances, 102-3, 153 n 19

Harlow, Clarissa (*Clarissa*), 66-67

Harris, James, 44-45, 47, 151 n 1

Hatlen, Burton, 63

Heathcliff, 9, 10, 70-75, 102, 103; as "absurd criminal," 107; as archetypal figure, 15, 70-75; and Catherine, 113; as demon-lover, 15,

70-75, 100; as Linton, 100; motivation, 113; as mythological figure, 11; as Satan, 99; similarity to Lovelace, 68-69; as vampire, 70-74; as victimizer, 114

Herd, David, 38

Hermes, 14, 23, 24

Hincmar, Archbishop of Reims, 55

Hitchcock, Alfred, 87

Hodgart, M.J., 35, 40, 46

Holt, Victoria, 56

"House Carpenter, The," 42, 151-52 n 8

Howels, Coral Ann, 55, 56, 58

Hughes, Douglas A., 87, 91

imprisonment, 9

incubi, 31, 33, 54, 55, 58, 61

James I (king of England), 30

Jameson, Frederick, 63

Jung, C.G., 25, 99; on *anima* and *animus*, 15; on archetypes, 5, 6, 13, 14; on "collective unconscious," 54, 99; compared to Freud, 5; and feminist criticism, 13-14; on fuction of myth, 5; on "individuation," 98; on "mother" archetype, 153 n 24; on projection, 19, 97-99, 112; on "shadow," 19, 114, 154 n 27

Kiessling, Nicolas, 54-55, 153 n 18

Klingopulos, G.D., 69

Kluger, Rivkah Schärf, 25

Kramer, Dale, 153 n 23

Laird, J.T., 154 nn 25, 29

Lamia, 58

Lang, Andrew, 42, 152 nn 13, 14; and "Demon Lover" ballad, 146-48

Lawrence, D.H., 7, 13, 80, 82, 84, 85, 86, 91, 100, 101, 114, 115; demon-lovers in fiction of, 81; "The

Lawrence, (*continued*)
Fox," 101; *Lady Chatterley's Lover*,
12; *The Virgin and the Gipsy*, 101;
*Women in Love*, 101
—"The Princess," 81, 103; as com-
pulsion tale, 80; and "Demon
Lover" ballad, 100; and demon-
lover motif, 89, 92, 100; motiva-
tion in, 108; obsession in, 89, 100,
114; rape in, 87; vow in, 83, 86.
*See also characters by name*
Laws, G. Malcolm, 38, 41-42, 69
Lessing Doris, 101, 103-4
Lewis, Matthew G., 55, 59
Linton. *See* Heathcliff
Linton, Edgar (*Wuthering Heights*),
10, 72, 99
Linton, Isabella (*Wuthering Heights*),
11, 74, 100, 107
Lockwood (*Wuthering Heights*), 70-
75
London blitz, 88
loneliness, 111
"Lord Lovel," 153 n 24
"Lord Randal," 153 n 24
"Lord Thomas and Fair Annet," 46
love, 8, 9, 18
Lovelace (*Clarissa*): as demon-lover,
15, 69, 110; Dracula compared to,
66; Eagleton on, 67-68; Fiedler on,
16; Heathcliff compared to, 69; as
literary prototype, 68

McAndrews, Elizabeth, 55
madness, 99
Mason, Bertha (*Jane Eyre*), 9
May, Rollo: on aggression and violence, 104-5, 106; on the demonic,
108; on *Love and Will*, 104, 108-9;
on power, 104-5; on projection,
112
Michelet, Jules, 151 n 5
misogyny, viii, 15
Modleski, Tania, 102, 103, 153 n 19
Motherwell, William, 38-39

myth, 92, 104; and ballads, 98, 151
n 1; and literature, 3; and myth-
makers, 4-5; mythological fiction,
18; mythological figures, 7, 14, 23
myth criticism, 6. *Also see* archetypal criticism

Narcissism, 112, 113
New Testament, 26, 29
nightmare, 4, 33
Norwood, Robin, 115-16

Oates, Joyce Carol, 101
obsession, 92, 102, 105; in "Demon
Lover" ballad, 69; in *Dracula*, 66;
as love and violence, 18; passion
as, 15; in "The Princess," 89, 100,
114; sexual, 65; in *Tess*, 69, 79; of
victims, 115; for a woman, 16; in
*Wuthering Heights*, 69, 75, 100
Old Testament, 25, 151 n 3
oppression, 14, 154 n 26; effect of,
12; literature of, vii; oppressor
and victim, 70, 104; social, 9; spiritual and psychological, 8; of
women, 9

Pan, 23-24, 29
passion, 8, 9, 11, 15
Peck, M. Scott, 109-11, 113-116, 154
n 27
Pepys, Samuel: Black-Letter ballads, 37; comparison of his "Demon Lover" with Scott's, 43-46;
and Thomas Percy, 38; "A Warning for Married Women," 41, 152
n 10
Percy, Thomas, 37, 38
persecution, 14
Pinion, F.B., 153 n 23
Plato, 32
Polidori, John Williams, 60
pornography, 151 n 2
power, 98, 105, 111, 117